MW01016706

REPORTING HOME

Olga Masters began her career in journalism at the
Cobargo Chronicle at the age of fifteen. Marriage and
seven children interrupted her career for many years, until
she returned to newspapers in the mid-1950s. Her first
collection of short stories, *The Home Girls*, was published in 1982, when she was sixty-three. It won a National Book Council Award. Masters died four years
later, having also written *Loving Daughters*, *A Long
Time Dying*, *Amy's Children*, and *The Rose Fancier*.

Deirdre Coleman is a graduate of the University of Melbourne, and has M.Phil. and D.Phil.degrees from Oxford University. She has been a lecturer at the universities
of Wollongong and Adelaide, and is now a lecturer in the
Department of English, University of Sydney. She has
published widely in the area of English Romanticism including a book on Samuel Taylor Coleridge's journalism,
Coleridge and "The Friend" 1809-1810, published by Oxford at the Clarendon Press, 1988.

By the same author

The Home Girls
Loving Daughters
A Long Time Dying
Amy's Children
The Rose Fancier

OLGA MASTERS

REPORTING HOME

Her writings as a journalist
Selected by Deirdre Coleman

University of Queensland Press

First published 1990 by University of Queensland Press
Box 42, St Lucia, Queensland 4067 Australia

Articles © Estate of the late C.F. and O.M. Masters 1990

Introductions, notes and selection © Deirdre Coleman 1990

This book is copyright. Apart from any fair dealing
for the purposes of private study, research, criticism
or review, as permitted under the Copyright Act, no
part may be reproduced by any process without written
permission. Enquiries should be made to the publisher.

Typeset by University of Queensland Press
Printed in Australia by The Book Printer, Maryborough

Distributed in the USA and Canada by
International Specialized Book Services, Inc.,
5602 N.E. Hassalo Street, Portland, Oregon 97213-3640

Creative writing program assisted by
the Literature Board of the Australia
Council, the Federal Government's arts
funding and advisory body

Cataloguing in Publication Data

National Library of Australia

Masters, Olga, 1919-1986.
Olga Masters: Reporting Home.

Bibliography.

1. Masters, Olga, 1919-1986 - Career in journalism. 2.
Women journalists - Australia. 3. Australia - Social life
and customs - 1945-   - Sources. I. Coleman, Deirdre. II. Title.

994.05

ISBN   0 7022 2265 8

For Gretta
In Memoriam Carmelina

CONTENTS

ILLUSTRATIONS

Following page 40

Postcard of Cobargo, New South Wales, in the 1920s
The Cobargo School of Arts
Cover of *Our Babies*, 1941
Women's page, *Northern Star*, 1962
Women's page, *Leader*, 1968
Women's page, *Land*, 1969
"My Boy Roy" article, *Manly Daily*, 1974
Cartoon for *Sydney Morning Herald* columns
Monet's *The Meadow*
Olga Masters, Tom Shapcott and Chris Wallace-Crabbe
Australian writers in Moscow

ACKNOWLEDGMENTS

This book is deeply indebted to my friend and colleague, Professor Dorothy Jones of the University of Wollongong, New South Wales. With her unerring skill in these matters, Dorothy was one of the first to recognise Masters as a major new talent on the Australian literary scene, and her scholarly articles on the fiction led the way in discussion of Masters' work. Many thanks also to the family of Olga Masters, particularly to her sister Del Miller and daughter Deb Masters, and to D'Arcy Randall and Helen Dash of University of Queensland Press.

On the secretarial front, Cindy Richardson and Marie Cominetti were a great resource, whilst Caroline Jasper, Vince Stefano and Matthew White were indefatigable fellow-diggers amongst old newspaper copy. Bronwen Levy and Susan Magarey gave advice and encouragement, Julie Lewis provided me with photographs of Cobargo, and Robin Eaden helped me to locate some of the illustrative material. Thanks are also due to the staff of the Mitchell Library, State Library of New South Wales, to Tom Shapcott for allowing me to see his unpublished "Russian Diary", and to freelance writer and broadcaster Kate Veitch who shared with me the radio tapes she had used for her "Coming Out Show: The Legacies of Olga Masters'', broadcast on ABC National Radio, September 1988.

Rosemary Dobson's poem "Country Press" is quoted from *Selected Poems* (North Ryde: Angus and Robertson 1973), by courtesy of Angus and Robertson.

For permission to use photographs and other illustrative material, thanks go to the *Northern Star*, the *St. George and Sutherland Shire Leader*, the *Land*, the *Manly Daily*, the *Sydney Morning Herald*, the *National Times,* and to the General Reference Library, State Library of New South Wales.

Editor's note

In order to achieve consistency of style in spelling and presentation, small changes have been made to Masters' articles. The paragraphing of the original newspaper columns has, however, been retained.

INTRODUCTION

> I was prompted to write on the theme of human relation-
> ships most likely through my dealing with people as a jour-
> nalist, since I wrote mostly human interest features. I always
> found the poor and humble to be the most interesting of my
> subjects, nearly always having the richest stories to tell.*

Olga Masters has been much celebrated as a late starter in
the field of writing. She was fifty-eight when she turned
her hand to playwriting and short fiction. Her first collection of stories, *The Home Girls*, was published in 1982
when she was sixty-three. Four years later she was dead,
leaving behind two collections of short fiction, three nov-
els, several unpublished plays, and almost thirty years of
journalism, a selection of which is presented in this vol-
ume.

The extraordinary belatedness of Masters' literary career has to some extent obscured the fact that she was a
seasoned journalist when she started to win prizes for her
fiction. Her career in journalism began early, at the age of
fifteen, and only ended with her death in 1986. After leaving school early to help out at home, she worked for a
brief time as a cadet on the *Cobargo Chronicle*, a weekly

* Olga Masters in *Contemporary Authors* (Detroit: Gale Research,
  1962-); vol. 121 (1987), 286-87.

newspaper serving the southern coastal area of New South Wales between Bega and Moruya. The year was 1934, the Great Depression squatted on the land, and Cobargo was the very dull place which later inspired the stories of small town life in *A Long Time Dying*. Her apprenticeship with the *Cobargo Chronicle*, a paper which advertised itself as devoted to "home" news, set the pattern for much of what was to come. Amidst advertisements for mechanical cream separators and other dairy machinery, Masters contributed anonymously to the Local and District News section. No item was too small for inclusion: the comings and goings of local people, their achievements, their mishaps, their anecdotes, their health — and even the health of their livestock. Rosemary Dobson, in her poem "Country Press", has captured the spirit of rural newspapers when she writes of the mythical *Western Star*:

> You say you have a notice? There's no one dies
> But what we know about it. Births, deaths and
> marriages,
> Council reports, wool prices, river-heights,
> The itinerant poem and the classified ads -
> They all come homewards to the *Western Star*. . .

Of course, in a newspaper of this kind it is impossible to identify anyone's contributions precisely, but that hardly matters in Masters' case. What is important is the realisation that these humble beginnings were to feed directly into her two later careers as a journalist and as a creative writer.

Although the editor of the *Cobargo Chronicle* encouraged her writing, he was often unable to pay his young assistant, and after several years of intermittent work on the paper, Masters was itching to get away to Sydney. She escaped, finally, in 1937, a courageous move for the eldest daughter of a large impoverished family. But for a young woman who did not have enough money to spend time looking for the work she wanted, there seemed limited opportunities in Sydney to continue her journalism, so she worked instead at jobs she hated, first as a shorthand typist, and later as a writer of advertising copy for radio. In 1940 she married, and for the next twenty years she was to live in small and large country towns in New South Wales, moving around with her schoolteacher husband Charles and their seven children from Ettalong to Grafton, to Urbenville and Lismore. It was not until 1955, when her eldest son Roy was fourteen, that she resumed her career as a journalist by working casually as a district correspondent, or "stringer", for the Lismore newspaper the *Northern Star*. At that time she was living in Urbenville, but when the family moved to nearby Lismore she took a part-time job with the paper, only finishing in the mid-1960s when she moved again, this time to Sydney. From this moment onwards until the end of her life, Masters was to work as a journalist on a succession of newspapers: the *St. George and Sutherland Shire Leader* (1966-69), the *Liverpool-Fairfield Champion* (1968-71), the *Land* (1969-71), the *Manly Daily* (full-time 1971-77, part-time 1979-83), and the *Sydney Morning Herald* (1984-86).

In numerous interviews, Masters paid tribute to her journalism as the long apprenticeship behind her sudden success. This apprenticeship was not grounded in the reporting of so-called "hard news" — the murders, fires and catastrophes which were, until recently, almost the exclusive terrain of male journalists. Sensational news stories such as these, which disrupted the routines and repetitions of daily life, were of no interest to Masters, and she used to be amused by colleagues who craved such incidents, remarking that "they were missing so much by overlooking the smaller things". These "smaller things" were to be found in the less newsworthy human interest assignments traditionally associated with the women's pages. None of the women's pages for which she worked concerned themselves with the activities of debutantes and socialites; rather, the staple of Masters' newspaper work was to report the Births, Deaths and Marriages of ordinary working people, the homely tales of wives, mothers and daughters, the successes and failures, the frustrations and triumphs of life in small communities. The reporting of commonplace events like these had, she claimed, greatly enriched her thinking about human nature and human behaviour. Those who sneered at the thought of covering a wedding provoked her to ask: "What is more important than a wedding?" Similarly, "You can't say 'how boring' about having to interview Girl Guides when guiding might be the most important thing in their lives".

Masters' sympathy with the thoughts and feelings of ordinary people was coupled with an intense curiosity, and it was this "terrifically inquisitive" instinct which made her a writer. According to Chris Masters, one of her sons, her career began, not when her first book was published, but when she started taking an interest in her neighbours. One of his strongest memories of his mother is of a woman walking to Manly beach from her house and never seeming to get there, such were the diversions ... stopping "every hundred metres" and coming back with "ten more stories she'd picked up along the way".

Provincial "neighbourhood" newspapers put this instinct for story telling to good use. Well aware of the blurred boundaries between fiction and journalism, Masters confessed that, when out on an assignment, she was often obliged to get a good story out of a few fragments. If the assignment finished in a dead end, the country reporter did not have the option of phoning in for another one: "You'd go out for a story and it wouldn't be much of a story, but you'd make it into a story. The lesson there was that there is more in life, more in situations, than meets the eye. The deeper you dig, the more you find." The writing of the short story "The Home Girls" illustrates this point. Whilst working on the *Manly Daily* in 1979 (the International Year of the Child), Masters interviewed a man who had been in charge of a children's home for forty years.* As he talked she realised that he had never, in all those years, given a thought to what went on inside the children's heads. This failure of insight provoked her to write "The Home Girls".

The continuity between journalism and fiction manifests itself in the desire to make a story, to develop the germ of a human interest assignment, no matter how unpromising at first sight, into an economical and satisfying narrative. The questions and answers of the interview become dialogue, some details are omitted whilst others are selected for highlighting, a particular point of view begins to emerge. Thus, journalism becomes the training ground in narrative techniques, teaching the writer how to take a situation and to develop it effectively; most importantly, when one considers the powerful economy of Masters' fiction, newspaper work taught her the value of the old journalistic adage on length: "Just give it what it's worth." There were also continuities of style and subject matter. The famously deceptive "simple style" of Masters' fiction arose directly from her long experience as a journalist. In fact, when asked to comment on the different approaches adopted for journalism and fiction, Masters denied that there was much difference: "I didn't find I had to change very much when I started to write fic-

---

* Interview unlocated — perhaps never published.

tion. I still wrote in a fairly simple, straightforward style, but I had this wonderful bonus of being able to describe, to indulge in a little description, that you couldn't do as a journalist." When she first began offering stories for publication this simple style occasioned her some anxiety because of the very sophisticated tribe of male writers currently in vogue: David Ireland, Murray Bail, Rodney Hall and Peter Carey. But despite the self-doubt, she was unable to make any fundamental alterations to her style; feeling herself to be too much of a late starter for experimentation with contemporary fashions in fiction, she consoled herself with the thought that after years of writing for the public she had, at the very least, earned her style.*

Masters' life spanned a period of enormous change in the structure and dynamics of the Australian family; and the lives of women past and present, within the home and outside it, form the principal subject matter of much of her journalism and fiction. Having grown up in the Depression in the countryside, she was acutely aware of the value of women's unpaid (and often unappreciated) labour in the home. The economic crisis forced poorer families like her own into a renewed dependence upon a local economy of home-produced food and clothing, and, of necessity, women were obliged to make do with extremely limited resources; in other words, the art of "home economics" became a matter of struggling to survive from day to day. Nor was the woman's maintenance of the family confined solely to material support. As we see in many of the short stories, such as "In Cobargo Now" (*A Long Time Dying*) and "The Sea on a Sunday" (*The*

*   Interview with Tom Thompson in *The View from Tinsel Town* (Southerly: Penguin, 1985), 42-46. Also, ABC Radio interview with Alison Cotes, 1985.

Home Girls), the effort of providing food and clothing
went hand in hand with the need to provide increased psychological support for unemployed, demoralised husbands and anxious, fearful children.

The experience of grinding poverty and hunger, and
the general hopelessness of that period, made an indelible
impression on Masters, one which she claimed stayed
with her for a long, long time, and influenced her writing.
The chief legacy was an awareness of the ways in which
the family—or "home"—failed to square with its ideol-
ogy as a purely private domain, offering refuge from the
stresses and strains of life outside. For Masters, the family unit was constantly subject to external forces, the most
important of which was, of course, the economy: "Always we're governed by the economy, our lives are struc-
tured by the economy." And while mothering had a
biological basis, it did not follow from this that there was
anything "natural" about the subordinate position of
women within the home, or the fact that so much of their
work was either invisible or undervalued. During the Second World War these points were to be driven home, so
to speak, when state governments set up creches and day-
care centres to enable some Australian women to leave
their traditional areas of employment and take up essential jobs to assist the war effort. The taste of liberation
given by increased pay and a position within the commanding economy was not a lesson quickly forgotten, although the postwar boom and the politically conservative
fifties conspired to put women back in their "proper
place".*

It is only with the recent burgeoning of feminist history

* Women's employment in essential war industries is discussed by
Constance Larmour in "Women's Wages and the WEB [Women's
Employment Board]", *Labour History 29* (1975): 47-58.

and sociology that attention has come to be focussed upon neglected areas of women's experience, and Masters' journalism — particularly her "Style" columns for the *Sydney Morning Herald* — needs to be read in that context. In many ways the "Style" columns make an important contribution to current feminist critiques of the modern Australian family. To speak of Masters as a feminist might arouse some resistance, but it was not a label she rejected. In 1985, when radio and newspaper interviewers quizzed Masters on her presentation of women in her first novel, *Loving Daughters*, she admitted she was a feminist and spoke passionately of injustices against women — the stifling of their talents, and the frustration and anguish they suffered when denied the right to express themselves.* A feeling for these injustices was, she claimed, central to *Loving Daughters* and was rooted in her own experience of growing up in the late 1920s. While Enid and Una were "bursting with talent ... the men in my story were very ordinary people — rather dull. The women were the brighter, and I think I saw that myself when I was growing up. I saw my own mother and aunts — how talented they were. But nobody ever asked their opinion of anything." Similarly, it was the aim of her story "The Teacher's Wife" to describe a female character "locked in a time-warp", a woman who had no choice but "to adjust her feelings and emotions to suit the environment and the lifestyle that were forced upon her".

Nor did Masters believe that the unfairness ended with that earlier era. Women still had to struggle to have their voices heard, they continued to be disadvantaged when mothering children, and the burden of housekeeping and domestic responsibility remained their undivided lot. Three "Style" columns explore these issues: "The loneli-

* ABC Radio interview with Alison Cotes, 1985.

ness of long-distance motherhood'', ''Don't forget, mothers are human beings too'' and ''Never fear, housewives—he's here''. The last is a biting attack on masculine presumption and selfishness, similar to that exhibited by the character George Carr in ''Brown and Green Giraffes'' (*The Rose Fancier*).

There can be little doubt that, consciously or unconsciously, the extraordinary profusion of domestic details and rituals in Masters' writing sprang from a desire to redress some of these injustices, even to celebrate areas of female experience formerly excluded from the domain of so-called ''serious'' literature. Obviously, as a wife and mother of seven children, home and the family had played a major part in her life, so much so, in fact, that when she ceased to be altogether housebound by returning to work in the mid-1950s, her journalist's eye inevitably viewed the world from the perspective of the living room and kitchen.

She was also returning to the anonymous reportage which she had written for the *Cobargo Chronicle* twenty years earlier. In the women's section of the *Northern Star*, alongside advertisements for diamond rings and bridal outfitters, she would have helped to compile those seemingly endless lists of engagement and wedding announcements, complete with their elaborately formulaic descriptions of the ring or the bride's dress. Once again it is impossible to identify and isolate her writing from that of other journalists assigned to these pages; nevertheless, a general picture emerges of the ends to which her energies must have been directed. Especially notable is the extraordinary profusion of detail in this era of white weddings: the engagement ring ''featuring a single diamond in the newest star setting with platinum bow filigree shoulders on a yellow gold band'', and the bride's ''three-tiered scalloped veil held by a coronet of nylon baby lilies with seed pearl centres". Sashes and posies, the bridesmaid's gown of "irridescent blue nylon chiffon over tafetta", even the Good Luck place cards at the reception, "designed by the bride's mother and decorated with silvered wish bones collected especially for the purpose" — all these minute details required a sharp and knowing woman's eye, similar to that which we later see emerging in the fiction, where one woman character observes "how the iron had been pressed with such force, the eyelet holes in the embroidery were large enough to see through", or where a fuji silk blouse with "a boat-shaped neck, finely bound, and sleeves eased gently into a similar binding at the elbow" comes to dominate an entire story ("A Spread of Warm Blood" in *A Long Time Dying*).

During the years that Masters worked for the *Northern Star*, the engagement and wedding lists were accompanied by a "Roundabout" column dedicated to the achievements of local women. Smaller items noted fashion parades, beauty contests, holidays, buffet teas, meetings of various hospital auxilaries and the Country Women's Association. A "District Personal" column also tracked the movement of locals backwards and forwards on their visits to and from relatives.

Two of the next three papers to employ Masters were the weeklies, the *St. George and Sutherland Shire Leader* and the *Land*. The *Leader* contained a "Women's News" section whose format did not differ greatly from that of the *Northern Star*, except that the "Social Round" column threw its net rather wider than the community catered for by the Lismore paper. As a suburban rather than country paper, shopping took a high profile, with a "Lucky Shopper" contest; in such a way did the newspaper serve its own interests and those of the business community whilst supposedly serving the interests of its women readers.

Reflecting, perhaps, the period during which Masters worked for the *Leader* (1966-69), the "Women's News" section gave quite a lot of space to the need for women to take an active role in community affairs. The Toastmistress Club, with its emphasis on the importance of public speaking, was one such organisation, as were also the VIEW clubs (Voice, Interest and Education for Women). At the same time, however, and the contradiction is writ large across all the papers on which Masters worked, these calls for a new assertiveness co-exist with full page features on engagement and wedding notices.

The *Land*, advertising itself as "Australia's leading rural weekly", took Masters back into the reporting of country life where notices of Cookery Contests, School Dinner Dances and Needlework Displays vied with each other for space in the "Woman's Interest" section. But a feature on the winner of the Mudgee scone-making finals might sit alongside an article on the Agriculture Department's appointment of two women officers to help the increasing number of women running the business side of their properties, a trend which paralleled the opening up in the early seventies of places for women at the major agricultural colleges. There was also a regular semi-fictional column called "Diary of a Country Mother", written by a woman called "Susie" from the central west of New South Wales. While the names of the people were fictitious, the incidents described purported to be the day-to-day experiences of the writer.

It was not until Masters went to work for the *Manly Daily* in the early 1970s that she wrote under her own name. The use of by-lines was a growing trend at this time, and it was a practice which helped to promote further the unusual community aspect of this suburban

daily. Situated on a peninsula, Manly has always had a
strong local identity, and this neighbourly aspect, together with the use of by-lines, suited Masters perfectly
because it gave scope to her powerful instinct for creating
a readership by fossicking out events and experiences "of
the kind people really like to read and with which they can
identify". The writing of human interest stories afforded
an important education in reader response, and her reso-
lute determination to give pleasure to readers quickly established her as a journalist much loved by the people of
Manly and nearby Warringah. In fact, since her death,
the *Manly Daily* has paid her work several tributes which
in themselves make little distinction between her contributions as a journalist and as a fiction writer. In 1987 it
founded an annual Olga Masters short story competition,
designed to provide encouragement and recognition for
new literary talent, and in 1988 the newspaper repub-
lished her 1974 feature article "My boy Roy" to coincide
with the launching of *The Rose Fancier*.

Masters' years at the *Manly Daily* were crucial to her
development as a writer. The short stories about modern
life which she began to write with such speed and urgency
in the late 1970s often owed the germ of their conception
to her human interest assignments; and even when the fictional settings moved back to the world of her childhood,
her prodigious memory was constantly exercised — even
triggered — by the similarities and dissimilarities of past
and present familial situations.

As a senior journalist for the *Manly Daily*, Masters
was very much her own boss. She re-designed the
women's page to suit her own needs, and worked tire-
lessly at covering the social issues which concerned her
most deeply; for instance, during 1979, the International
Year of the Child, she wrote a staggering number of articles about homeless and foster children in the Manly-

Warringah area. She also never ceased to champion the struggle of working wives and mothers. Although acutely aware of the need to see the family as necessarily subject to larger cultural and political forces, she strongly supported women who defended their families against outside intervention, particularly against the tribes of "experts" — the professional doctors and psychologists, social workers and child care specialists. In one article she tells the story of a mother whose loving devotion to her Down's syndrome child confounded the experts, almost all of whom claimed the little girl would never live a "normal" life. The story (12 June 1981), accompanied by a photo of mum watching her daughter set off for her first day at primary school, is in some respects a latter-day retelling of Emily Russell's devotion to her "crompy" child Dorothy in "Tea with Sister Paula" (*A Long Time Dying*).

Masters' concern over the negativism or interference of the state in family life is best seen in her humorous article for *New Parent* magazine, "Once upon a time . . .". In this autobiographical account of mothering she dramatises the conflict in the 1940s between natural, common-sensical childcare and the new scientific principles institutionalised by childcare professionals. The particular object of her attack is the textbook *Our Babies*, which was issued by the New South Wales Department of Public Health in 1931 and still enjoyed a wide circulation throughout the forties and fifties. Although independent-minded mothers like herself defied these new "rational" principles of feeding by the clock and weaning by the calendar, it was difficult not to feel undermined and anxious in the face of such institutionalised attempts at external control.

Masters wrote, and compiled, much of the routine work of the women's pages, keeping her *Manly Daily* readers up to date with local and national domestic news. National Mothering Week gets advance publicity, as does National Nursing Home Week and Red Cross Calling Month. The Lovely Motherhood Quest, a local charity event featuring a fashion parade of neck-to-knee swim suits, offers a welcome parody of other beauty contests, and the "Diary Dates" section chronicles local charity socials, dinners, theatre parties, street stalls and concerts. By definition, hack work of this kind is undistinguished, and Masters' was no exception, but the chronicling of sections such as the "Diary Dates" was a way of keeping in touch and an obvious source of the human interest stories which she so much enjoyed writing. There was only one aspect of the women's pages she disliked, and that was the writing of fashion editorials and advertising copy. Since most newspapers derive between sixty and seventy per cent of their income from advertisements, and small papers have no separate advertising staff and sales department, the job of puffery was an inescapable one, but that did not stop Masters (and other journalists) from resenting this appropriation of their skills. For Masters in particular, adverse to fashion and consumerism, the artificial creation of wants through advertising must have rubbed very much against the grain.

For the most part, Masters' human interest stories focus on women engaged in all sorts of activities and aspirations, from bus drivers to company directors to the young woman with her new phone-a-cake business. Many are witty, such as the story of the Indian bride who, after arriving in Australia, served her husband twenty-six different main course dishes in as many days. A passion for cooking would have appealed to Masters; doubtless she was also intrigued by the later entrepreneurial extension of this traditional bride's domesticity into cooking classes for the public. Other articles chronicle the most mundane of domestic routines, some of which are to re-surface in the fiction, such as the pouring of dish-washing water on the backyard's lemon tree ("Leaving Home" in *The Home Girls*). On more serious matters, an underwear shop is featured because it caters for women who have had mastectomies; and a survivor of the terrors of post-natal depression pays tribute to women from the Companion Roster who pulled her through the crisis, not by offering marital or psychological counselling but simply by their presence and help in the home.

The quickly changing patterns of women's lives fascinated Masters, and much of her effort went into providing essential information as to where and when women in the local community could obtain help and advice as they contemplated new departures from domestic routine. Mature women who want to go back to study but need encouragement as to how to combine their aspiration with housework, or a job in office or factory, are informed of the relevant open day, while those seeking to adopt children are reminded of the existence of an Adoptive Parents Association of New South Wales. The issue of adoption was one which reflected the huge changes in traditional family patterns, with birth control, more readily available abortion, and more tolerant attitudes towards single mothers depleting the number of available babies. In this particular case, Masters' strategy is to convey the facts simply and without comment, but in articles where an interviewee voices strong opinion, she often counters with a view from the other side. One such article (25 March 1981) was based around the claim of a church welfare officer that the incidence of family breakdown in the Manly-Warringah area was one of the highest in Sydney. Masters gives scope to the welfare worker's diagnosis that people do not work at marriage any longer because they are too busy pursuing "instant gratification", but the article does not end where the welfare officer would have it — in placing the blame for family breakdown on women who want to go out to work before their children have grown up. Immediately after reporting this claim, Masters adds that "the pressure of two parents working, or one parent working at two jobs contributed to stress and family breakdown. Women's roles were changing more rapidly than men's and husbands were not taking their full share of responsibility within the family." Although it is not stated explicitly by Masters, the "one parent working at two jobs" could of course be a mother trying to combine housework with paid employment.

The *Manly Daily* articles vary in length but rarely exceed six hundred words. The limited space was sufficient for the community service aspect of her work, but, as she admitted in an interview, "it was often frustrating to go on a news story, meet a fascinating person and be restricted to writing six paragraphs". For a woman who had always wanted to write, these frustrations would in themselves have been cause enough to lay down her journalistic pen, but there was also a strong sense of time running away. So, towards the end of 1977, she stopped work for the *Manly Daily* and turned her attention to writing radio and stage plays. One of her plays was broadcast by the ABC in 1978, and it was in that year that she also wrote her first short story, "The Snake and Bad Tom". Other stories followed quickly, and with the acceptance of one of them for the *Sydney Morning Herald* she felt herself to be in full stride. By 1981 she was back at the *Manly Daily* part-time, although she had already won no less than nine prizes for her short fiction, including the prestigious award — shared with Elizabeth Jolley — of the South Pacific Association for the Study of Language and Literature. It was only in 1983, when she received her first grant from the Literature Board of the Australia Council, that she ceased her part-time work in Manly.

The world of journalism did not sit complacently by and watch Masters retire from the field. By January 1984 moves were afoot to secure her for the *Sydney Morning Herald*, and her first article — "Things I'd love to do before I die" — appeared in December of that year. At that time Thomas Keneally was an occasional columnist for the *Herald*, and it seemed to Masters that significant changes were taking place in the newsprint world, with journalists being given greater scope to experiment with different modes of writing. But the perception of change was perhaps more an indication of her own greatly altered circumstances than anything else, for she was now an established and recognised writer, sought after by one of Australia's most powerful newspapers. The fact that she looked forward to collecting her columns into a book is a measure of how far she had come from the anonymous and routine work of previous years.

Most of the journalistic pieces collected in this book are "Style" columns written for the *Sydney Morning Herald* in 1985 and 1986. Here, for the first time, we see Masters writing outside the format of the women's pages. Chronicling and record keeping, the human interest assignments which she valued so highly — all these give way to "opinion" on topics as diverse as writing, reading, art, Soviet literature, the Second World War, housekeeping and the latest fads and fashions. That she wrote for the "Style" section is something of an irony, since she was at best ambivalent about change, and many of her opinions are distinctly unstylish. Upholding a world of old-fashioned, working-class values, she uses nostalgia as a weapon against bourgeois affluence and the consumer society. Material prosperity seemed to sit uneasily on the generation which grew up during the Depression and the war years; long inured to the impossibility of fulfilling desires and dreams, the later easy purchase of a new iron, a new dress, an overseas holiday, brought little satisfaction. Thus, in Masters' own marvellous image, while the Depression came and "hung about like an unwanted guest", it never really vanished from the home it had visited, so that, in after years, one's entire way of seeing was haunted by its presence.

Readers of Masters' fiction will encounter a new and different voice in these columns. Instead of the powerfully ironic restraint and reticence of her fictional narrative, we hear the voice of social comment, most often humorous, but sometimes overtly moralistic and wilfully optimistic. Of course she was "writing down" to an extremely narrow space of eight hundred words, and the exploration of painful or disturbing topics had necessarily to be confined; but it is also true that the face she wanted to present to the world was that of an incorrigible optimist. For instance, she hated the thought that readers might be struck by the hopelessness of the situations and characters she described in her fiction. The very title *A Long Time Dying* was, she argued, expressive of the hope in human nature; despite the harshness of conditions in the 1930s, people were survivors: "They made the best of what was available to them, limited as it was."* Many readers of *A Long Time Dying* might find these claims rather extraordinary; certainly her own children were astonished by the awesome power of their mother's stories, her tough-minded refusal to soften or sentimentalise painful and hopeless situations.

There were many contradictions in Masters' life of writing. She was often quoted as saying that her seven children were her finest books, and yet she dedicated

* ABC Radio interview with Pru Goward, 1985.

Amy's Children to them, a novel about a woman who simply abandons her children in order to find an identity for herself. Similarly, although much of her writing celebrates the home and women's domestic creativity, the futile snapping of Una's scissors in the air in *Loving Daughters* lingers with the reader as an image of thwarted creativity. But most subversive of all was her ironic description of two displaced, homeless children as "The Home Girls", and her later claim that we are all home girls at heart. When a reporter went to interview her in 1983, Masters had firm ideas about the image of herself she wanted to present to the reading public. Mischievously, she kept on urging the reporter to photograph her as a home girl in the kitchen, making a cake.*

Masters never lost her sense of humour. True to the maxim "once a journalist, always a journalist", she joked, when dying: "William Faulkner wrote a book called *As I Lay Dying*. The bastard scooped me." And in one of her last short stories, "Here Blue", it is as though she were carrying forward the history of Cobargo and its defunct newspaper into the late 1970s. Set in a dingy town overtaken by the motorcar, Andy Walters, editor of the failing *Pine Valley News*, might well be the ghost of Andy Wallace, editor of the *Cobargo Chronicle* when Masters was a cadet:

> Andy had had a good bi-weekly newspaper once, and a reporter helping him. Now it was a monthly double sheet which he wrote and laid out and sent to printers in Newcastle. He distributed it himself from his old car. At some Pine Valley houses the last two or three issues would be lying sodden and discoloured in gutters and long grass. The columns had less and less advertising in them and more and more of

* Interview with Deborah Tarrant, the *Weekend Australian Magazine*, 15-16 October 1983.

Andy's two line pleas to shop locally and support the local paper.

"Ah, it's not like the old days, is it?" Molly said, opening the till and slamming it shut after checking its empty state.*

In the playful colloquialism which ends this story about a backward girl and her dog—"Pine Valley was surely going to the dogs"—we hear at one and the same time the fiction writer and the populist, punning journalist.

Deirdre Coleman

* From "Here Blue" in *The Rose Fancier* (St Lucia: UQP, 1988).

— *The*
Manly Daily

99,000 READERS DAILY

26 Sydney Road, Manly, 2095   977 3333 (15 lines). Night Ads, 977 3246.

Vol. 67. No. 16,120.   SATURDAY, JUNE 22, 1974.   PRICE 5c

MY BOY ROY

The first article presented here, a Saturday feature
which became popularly known as ''My boy Roy'',
played an important part in strengthening Olga
Masters' resolve to write fiction. The editor of the **Manly
Daily** wanted her to write a humorous piece about the
Manly versus Penrith match, from the biased point of
view of the mother of Roy Masters, coach of the Penrith
side. After some demurring, Masters agreed, and
eleven years later she was still marvelling at the ''absolutely unbelievable response'' it provoked:

> People rang all next day, and they laughed, and some of
> them almost cried. One man said to me, ''Oh, I remember
> the oranges''. And I thought, gee, I've made that man re-
> member something from long, long ago. That's what
> writing's all about. It's reaching people through words;
> and not so much what you say, but what it makes them
> think of. That story started me. That made me think, well,
> look, I really will have a go. Surely I'm ready now to do
> something. Shortly after that I took two years off to try my
> hand at fiction.

The high-spirited humour of this feature (which appeared under the heading ''Mummulgum's proudest
mum goes to the Manly match . . . and she took
along a batch of rock cakes (not for throwing at the Eagles)'') stems largely from its burlesque of backpage
male sports reporting, a genre sacred to Australian

journalism and to the Saturday edition of newspapers. Readers' expectations are rudely reversed: at first it appears as though sports news has made it onto the front page, but a reading of the article gives no news at all about Thursday's match between Manly and Penrith. The game is, in fact, nowhere to be seen; centre field has been usurped by a reporter-mum with oranges and rock cakes, steadfastly clinging to her tender, doting, simple-minded view of the sport: would the boys really want to munch rock cakes after the game when they could be guzzling beer? All in all, it is a highly successful narrative. The mother's point of view is consistently dramatised, the son's rugby jargon highlights the absence of football at the centre of the piece, and the nostalgia for bygone Mummulgum days and six-stone footballers was guaranteed to strike a sympathetic chord with mums and dads on both sides of the Manly-Penrith divide.

Four days later, Masters followed up the feature article with her recipe for success, reprinted here as ''Olga's rock cakes''.

My boy Roy

Manly Daily, 22 June 1974

Mummulgum's proudest mum goes to the Manly match . . . and she took along a batch of rock cakes (not for throwing at the Eagles)

All the male reporters were down with 'flu on Thursday and there was a threat that no one would be available to report the Manly-Penrith match at Brookvale Oval.

Late in the afternoon the editor suggested I go along.

This came as a great surprise, because I did not know

anyone in the office was aware of my affiliation with big rugby league through my boy Roy.

Wisely I keep my personal life to myself, and had never mentioned that my boy Roy took the triumphant Australian schoolboy rugby league team to England in 1972 and his brilliant coaching resulted in their line being crossed only once in the thirteen-match tour.

He came back to take a national coaching examination with a distinction, and joined the Penrith club as a coach for the premiership 1974 season.

When told of my assignment I flew to the phone to make yet another illegal call to Penrith.

Roy told me not to worry; he would fill me in on the game and explain such quaint phrases like scrum going down, finding touch, and so on.

In fact he said he could tell me the score then.

"With Ashurst kicking, Stephenson getting most of the ball, Glen West running like a deer, Walton taking every goal, we should be jake."

"We should be level at halftime," said my boy Roy.

"The last two points in the last five minutes of play could go either way. Probably ours."

I went home and baked a batch of rock cakes for him to share with the team on their ride home to Penrith after the match.

I took the tin to him in the coach's box at the start of the game.

This was a disappointment. I thought he would be in his blue coach's gear — a perfect match for his eyes — but he was in an orange-coloured shirt, tweed sports coat and brown pants, and looked like an ordinary person.

I went and sat close to the oval and my thoughts went back over the years to the days when he was in the six-stone team at Mummulgum.

Then a thought hit me.

Oranges! Where were the oranges?

At Mummulgum we mothers used to go on after the game with oranges cut into quarters and hand them out for the players to suck to ease their parched throats.

I left the ground and ran a mile along Pittwater Road, to find a fruit shop.

There were people inside with glazed eyes, and foolish grins on their faces, and the one with a radio going full blast.

One moved forward to serve me, like he was in a trance.

"Hamilton is back in form . . . Eadie is brilliant . . . there's no holding them now . . . we'll make it to the finals."

These names were unfamiliar to me, so they must have been following another code of football—perhaps the World Cup Soccer series—as they were New Australians.

I ran back to the ground with my oranges.

An interested bystander looked at me counting them out on the seat.

"You won't need one for Ashurst, lady," he said. "He's been sent off!"

I wheeled round and looked for Big Bill, who only a couple of weeks ago had cooked a steak for me at a Penrith barbecue.

I could not see his amiable lumbering figure and his darling black head.

"Why, oh why?" I cried.

"Rough play, luv."

He wouldn't have meant it.

Out there on that cold, bleak field he would have been homesick for the chaffinch singing in the orchard bough in England now and, in passion of loneliness, he must have flayed the air with his great arms and accidentally hit someone.

I turned back dumbly to the oranges.

I had no knife to cut them into quarters, like we did in Mummulgum.

But my boy Roy, as well as everything also, was a Queen's Scout in his youth and he always carried his six-bladed knife, adding in recent years a corkscrew — through association with some of the rougher types — inevitable unfortunately, in the process of reaching adulthood.

I raced to the coach's box.

I asked for the loan of his knife.

"Don't Mum, don't!" he cried.

"Don't cut your throat until the game is over . . . the final score on the board. I'm hanging on to hope. You can too."

I went back to my place and naturally had to have my back to the field to cut up the oranges.

But I kept my ear on the game, as it were, through the spectators around me.

I knew we must have been winning because they were all Manly supporters and were yelling, "Kill the bastards."

These are the kind of things said at the height of a passionate desire to see Manly win — an understandable attitude, with opposition like Penrith.

I put the cut-up oranges back into the bag to take them to Roy.

I raced after him into the dressing shed because it appeared that, as the players were coming off, the game was over.

Someone rudely tried to shut the door in my face.

"Get out lady," said this large burly man. "They're changing."

This was ridiculous.

My boy Roy was in there and I had seen him without his clothes hundreds of times.

Besides, I had to ask him which side took the last two points.

Olga's rock cakes

Manly Daily, 26 June 1974

Quite a few people asked following the piece in last Saturday's *Manly Daily* about the Manly-Penrith rugby league match, if the Panthers really ate up the rock cakes I made for them.

I was assured they did. These delicious fruity little morsels are best washed down with piping hot tea or steaming coffee.

My boy Roy (if you read Saturday's article carefully you will find a mention of him as the Panthers' coach), evaded questions on what liquid refreshment washed them down on the trip home to Penrith.

But I am sure the players' mums saw to it they had flasks of tea and coffee packed with their change of jersey to help keep out the cold.

Rock cakes were a great favourite with the Mummulgum teams.

Occasionally, we saw fit to withhold some from players who let the side down.

Here is the recipe:

Sift three cups of self-raising flour with a pinch of salt. Rub in three tablespoons of butter very thoroughly. Add three tablespoons of castor sugar. Grate the rind of a lemon and add that.

Scatter into the mixture a handful of sultanas, and about half that amount of currants. Make a well in the centre and mix in two eggs beaten with enough milk to make a soft dough. Drop dessertspoonsful on to a greased slide, placing a piece of curled candied lemon peel on each. Bake in a moderate oven about thirty-five minutes.

This makes about twenty-six—two each for the team.

Raspberry slice was another tasty treat for the Mummulgum lads.

They are best cut into squares when they come from the oven, and allowed to travel in the tin without disturbance.

For the base, you need to rub two tablespoons of butter into two scant cups of sifted self-raising flour.

Add one tablespoon of castor sugar, a pinch of salt and a beaten egg to make a dough.

Spread on the base of a greased lamington tin. Spread generously with raspberry jam. Mix together a large cup of coconut, half a cup of sugar, half a teaspoon of vanilla and a beaten egg. Some melted butter makes this topping richer. Spread it over the jam, and bake in a moderate oven till cooked and nicely browned.

CREATIVITY

Masters' life of writing was so closely bound up with her life in the home that domesticity itself becomes the principal analogue for her thinking about the creative process. Writing was, she claimed, like making a garden or making a dress; it could also be compared to cooking, and it is this analogue which she develops in her article, "Slow combustion on a hot typewriter". With deft humour she conjures up the lulls and frustrations of creativity such as the tendency of narrative to defy authorial control, a legacy, perhaps, of what she claimed was the ingrained journalistic habit of disregarding plot in favour of taking a situation or a set of characters and simply allowing them to develop. Domesticity could also offer an undisciplined escape from the rigours of writing; one of her reasons for rising at the unsociable hour of 4.30 a.m. was the impossibility of abandoning her typewriter in order to turn on the vacuum cleaner. Similarly, her experience as writer-in-residence at the Fremantle Arts Centre in June-July 1985, just a few months before the "Slow combustion" article appeared, taught her that "you don't need to take breaks—it's better to write on and untangle the knots at the typewriter than wander around the paddocks or bake a cake to get yourself out of that writer's block we hear so much about". She was also busy warning her creative writing students in Fremantle to avoid the "great authors" and concentrate on their own strengths instead: "Who," she asked, "wants to go home with a deflated ego after a helping of Chekhov?"

The childhood which she invokes in "Slow combustion" as the unfallen time of purely pleasurable reading re-emerges in her reflections on the French impressionist painting **The Meadow**. Here, in a delightfully unashamed Australian appropriation of Monet's European scene, she locates an image of her own rebellious art, with its focus on ordinary, common people.

Slow combustion on a hot typewriter

Vogue Australia, September 1985

Creativity's a fragile essence, not to be ruined by good example

Reading, for a writer, is like going out to dinner after working all day as a chef.

In the restaurant the chef has half an eye on the clock, the other half on his assistants, half the other eye on the recipe or turned into his mind where the ingredients and measurements are recorded, and you can be sure there is plenty for the other half eye to do.

He is probably never completely satisfied with his finished dish. He would have liked a little more time, fresher mushrooms perhaps, and some fool apprentice made a dent with his thumb in the cheese crusted potatoes.

When the food has gone to the table he is ready to throw off his cap, fling away his starched coat and finish off the brandy the same fool apprentice forgot to add to one of the sauces.

At home he gets into comfortable pants and the check flannel shirt he's so fond of, and goes to his good friends Anna and Tom who have slaved for hours to make a late dinner for three.

Now he is out to enjoy himself. He has earned his treat. He is in the right frame of mind to be generous with praise for the good parts of the fare and silent (but gratified) at the doubtful ones. (He is pretty sure he will find a couple of pips in the lemon soufflé.) Anna and Tom are nervous. Perhaps they overdid the herbs in the Welsh rarebit. They avoid watching him eat.

"Isn't it great?" they say to each other when he has gone. "Louis is so wrapped up in his craft, yet he is able to appreciate the work of other cooks." They refrain out of modesty from saying *good* cooks.

A writer (like a chef) is seldom in complete control of his work. Characters go off on tangents of their own, defying the plot, images fail to rise from the dustiest corner of the room, faces wear blank expressions, voices speak stilted, unnatural dialogue. At such times the writer crawls to the nearest couch or chair and takes up a book to see how the other fellow made out.

Given this frail state, the book needs to be chosen carefully. A book one couldn't possibly have written but would have loved to, or one you might have written but didn't, would do nothing to soothe your jangled nerves.

You would dodge a book such as John Updike's *Couples*. That wretched man took ten couples (ten no less) in that New England village (a dead ringer for your corner of suburbia) never once confusing the reader so that he or she had to turn pages back to check the lawful partners of Carol and Foxy and Angela and Janet and all the others when they became mismatched as the story progressed. He dropped into his pages such delightful gems, you can forgive him while he insists you read every line in order that you get all of them in their right houses — furnished, you must concede, exactly as their characters dictate.

For instance: "The children's choir singing, an unsteady theft of melody while the organ went on tiptoe, ceased. In silence the ushers continued their collection of rustles and coughs." The fellow has been everywhere, even in church.

No one should be fooled by a writer crying out in (phoney) ecstasy "I am dying to read the new Salman Rushdie!" (Or Garner, or Jolley, or Malouf.)

Death may come in the form of the shock of finding the writing infinitely superior to one's own, the subject as foreign as a language never learned. (How does a tone deaf writer cope with a Jolley or a Garner, who are plainly as skilled with a piano and harpsichord as with a pen?)

A writer nervously plucking at the bookshelves for diversion, her own work shrouded beneath the typewriter cover like a half-made dress turning out badly, will avoid Henrik Ibsen if working on a play, and dodge *A World of Great Stories* if bent on a collection of short fiction.

Who but Ibsen could have Nora slam a door so tellingly in *A Doll's House?* Who else but the American Ben Hecht could capture a snow storm as in his short story *Snowfall in Childhood?* Listen to his beginning: "I got out of bed and saw what happened to the night." Sometimes, a single opening sentence could be put between two hard covers and it would be enough.

"It was the best of times," Charles Dickens wrote at the start of *A Tale of Two Cities*. Those half-dozen words could start a hundred stories. But Dickens got in first. "The night belonged to the novelist" opened *Miss Peabody's Inheritance* succinctly for Elizabeth Jolley.

Childhood is perhaps the one time in a writer's life when total involvement, total enjoyment comes from reading. Too early then to be smitten by the writing bug, books are devoured as hungrily as chocolate bars. (The taste lingers and turns them into writers.)

I remember reading *David Copperfield* on the tank-stand of St Joseph's Convent in Cobargo, New South Wales, pressed between the veranda railing and the corrugated iron tank, trying to keep private my weeping at the death of David's mother. I counted the hours until I could rush home, fling myself on my astounded mother and beg forgiveness for throwing my boiled egg at my brother that morning. I spent the hours until bedtime crushed to her side while she tried to get tea for the ten of us, to convince myself she was alive and unlikely to languish soon on a deathbed.

Among the best reading for a writer is writing about writers. In David Cecil's *Portrait of Jane Austen,* Ms Austen is said to have assigned herself the task of making breakfast, a not inconsiderable job if all the Austens, five boys and two girls, were home at once. Morsels such as this are highly digestible to a writer with a guilt complex about abandoning the typewriter too often for the comfort of cooking pots.

Biographers claim that Katherine Mansfield got very little writing done until the postman came with the day's mail. (Did she, too, nervously await rejection slips?)

I found Frank Kenyon's story of George Eliot, *The Consuming Flame,* boring and unconvincing — except for a couple of lines: "Marian [George] has also begun a novel, but feeling unsure of herself has abandoned that too."

One wonders about the chef's reading if he finds sleep evading him, perhaps a legacy of Anna's heavy hand with the herbs, or the uncertainties of tomorrow when the apprentice may do worse than forget to add the brandy and fail to turn up for work. He is bound to have more cook-books on hand than any other kind. Some authors of these give more than recipes. Their writing comes out as rich and smooth as their bechamel sauce. And with the right touch.

Margaret Fulton in the best selling *Margaret Fulton Cookbook* writes forewords such as: "What wonderful memories I have of soup and my Scottish mother's kitchen. We had soup every day, each one had its own character and charm. My mother would rather use cream to enrich fish or tomato soup than pour it over peaches."

Chefs (and writers) may be intimidated by the skills of their counterparts. But there is comfort in the kinship.

Monet exhibition: *The Meadow*

Sydney Morning Herald, 15 June 1985

Bourgeois and irreverent as it sounds I think of a certain cartoon many times when I am drawn to a famous painting. This cartoon depicts a politician viewing a picture and offering the time-worn quote: "I know nothing about art, but I know what I like." He is looking at a portrait of himself.

Looking at *The Meadow* one sees oneself, the child, the adult, the familiarity of time and place.

The village is French, the dress of Monet's time when he was middle-aged towards the end of the nineteenth century.

But it could be New England in New South Wales with the poplars and the church spires and the light of early afternoon.

The adults are at the edge of the meadow, one with a parasol. She does not trust the elements but the children rushing forward see no danger, no risk of a sudden downpour of rain, no sunstroke, no snake or spiders.

They would throw off their restricting clothing and hampering hats if they dared but this would impede their escape.

"Back here at once!" the mothers would scream, or use a more suitable French term. Then the children would have to turn and deny us the exuberance on their faces, and Monet's brush would have gone still on the canvas, like his trees and houses and churches and sky. They would have to be retied of shoelace and hair ribbon and grass seeds plucked from muslin and ordered to remain close to their peers and wear chastened expressions, while the peers were allowed to look as lofty and disdainful as they liked.

Afterwards at nursery tea of mutton broth and croutons, the mothers are contrite. "We know it was only a little romp in the meadow but we love you and don't want anything to happen to you."

But what they really say is: We don't want adventure for you. We want security. We want you still and safe with us. (And like us.)

Monet put roads in his painting, a network of them. The children want nothing of them. Their backs are turned on them. Man-made, they are only for straight and narrow feet.

Perhaps they see a circus ahead. The edge of a village is just the place to set one up. The colours are brighter than the yellow flowers through which they plunge. Or, if there is no circus, one could come any moment.

Drawn to a painting, impressed by this master impressionist, a question is raised. Why the attraction to *The Meadow?*

Monet the rebel is there in his painting. He broke away from tradition, cast off restrictions imposed by art circles and went out and painted people, ordinary ones in all the different lights. He kept his ethereal or spiritual influence but he made his people real, liking them better than cathedrals, trains, boats and waterlilies.

He met opposition when he dared make change. But, like his running children, he didn't want only to admire the flowers in the meadow but get among them. And to search for something better, believing it to be there.

His parents opposed his ideals, chastised him, punished him. He is both the running child and (most likely when his turn came) the parent imposing his own set of restrictions on his own children.

We like what is familiar, what we understand. What is us.

The politician looking at his own portrait in approval was not that far out after all.

The Cobargo Chronicle

VOL. XII. — NO. 572. DECEMBER 24, 1909. SINGLE COPY 6D.

NOSTALGIAS

The startling power of Olga Masters' memory is re-
vealed in her autobiographical columns dealing with
old days and old ways. She evokes details, objects
and rituals long forgotten: broken teacups, shiny linoleum, the iceblock delivered around the back of the
house, the tin of Arnott's biscuits, and the open and
shared communal space of the old-fashioned veranda—a place from which, in blurring the boundaries
between "home" and "not home", one can survey
the world and be surveyed in turn.

The article "Once upon a time . . ." was commis-
sioned by **New Parent** magazine, the official journal of
Parents Centres Australia. Describing itself as a for-
ward-thinking journal offering support and information to those wishing to make informed decisions about
birth and parenting, **New Parent** champions the
"natural" instinctive care of infants and children over
the intervention of a professional, predominantly
male, medical establishment. One of its major contributors is a mother with a doctorate in psychology, and
in general the articles are aimed at a readership well-
informed in both medical and cultural terms. Ostensi-
bly feminist and radical in its insistence that women
accept the validity of their own experiences in defi-
ance of the professionals, the emphasis on what is
"natural" leads some of its contributors to a passion-

ately conservative stance on childcare and working mothers. Masters does not, in her article, discuss the often contentious subject of working mothers, confining her comments instead to the earliest years of infancy. Certainly, her article is entirely sympathetic to the journal's feminist valorisation of women's experience, and in a publication devoted to the most up-to-date technology of the "natural", her witty reminiscences of child-rearing in the forties offered **New Parent** readers something new and different.

Things I'd love to do before I die

Sydney Morning Herald, 1 December 1984

Great theatre, books, buildings, art and music I would like to revisit (having not taken a good enough look the first time) or freshly experience?

In my lifetime? Actually go there?

I would need to be hasty about it. As it is I twitch if away from the typewriter for twenty consecutive minutes.

I began writing at fifty-eight. That was seven years ago. I have mini nightmares about the time I have left, whether there is enough of it to write down all I want to. It's quite tantalising. A character comes up in a chapter of my current work and I dream for a short while (a very short while) of weaving a whole book around him/her. That would be the book after the book after the book I'm doing.

I see myself sans teeth, hearing, sight, dragging an arthritic body to a word processor, the ear-piercing snapping sound of my knuckles cracking with the effort of finding the joints of my fingers.

So I'll set aside a couple of days only to revisit the theatre, building, art and music of my far-off youth.

Cobargo in southern New South Wales is the place.

The School of Arts was the local theatre where St Joseph's Convent school once staged a concert. I learned that time a lesson about life I never forgot.

The concert was pure magic, the rag and paper costumes passing for rich silks and brocades under the dim kerosene lights, all those pale discs that were parents' faces tipped back in soundless adulation.

It made us kick higher, twirl more wildly and raise voices loud enough to lift the tin roof and shake the cobwebs from the windows.

It wasn't only the concert either. There was next day at school, singled out for praise by the nuns, who had the awesome task of supervising every act but keeping out of the public eye, obeying church doctrine.

Immediately after the last act our father whisked us away home. The advantage here was saving us the humiliation of departing in a sulky in a line-up of Fords, Buicks, Studebakers and Austins of better-off families.

So we missed the ice cream.

In a burst of generosity and pride a good Catholic parent ordered a churn full from the town's only cafe and ladled it out backstage to the cast minus the luckless Lawlers (us).

I learned then there is never a perfect whole, life is not as smooth and sweet as ice cream, a sour edge is bound to creep in.

The main Cobargo store will do for a great building. I believe it is gone now but then, around 1930, it was a joy to enter. The dark beams made it dim, and the floor seemed always newly scrubbed. There was the smell of soap and eucalyptus, cinnamon and sweets. The biscuits were in large square tins—Arnotts only. The storekeeper would take a knife and slide it around the edge of the tin, breaking the paper covering with a sound like a trumpet calling you to a great banquet.

For art there was my brother's drawing of the Cobargo Agricultural and Horticultural show president, who was also the storekeeper and biscuit tin opener, exhibited at the annual show.

I stayed by it in the pavilion where it hung, to hear what people had to say, and my father stood by the compositions in the schoolwork section written by my sisters and me to make sure that everyone read them. My mother, who believed praise in large doses was sinful, was halfway down the hill giving the baby what she called a good long sleep. She also feared for repercussions, like cutting off our credit, if the storekeeper took offence at his exaggerated chin in my brother's drawing. (Remember all of you, this was the peak year of the Great Depression.)

I regret the music. I'm tone deaf and any tickets to the great music bowls of the world would be wasted on me.

But ah, the books. The Cobargo School of Arts did not have a library that I recall, so I discovered literature late, but thankfully not too late.

So whisk me off to the deep American South (I will spare a week somehow) and let me walk in Flannery O'Connor country.

She died at thirty-nine, after writing some of the world's best short stories. She lived most of her life on a dairy farm run by her mother and wrote mainly about the neighbouring dirt farms. There is magic in her description of a simple sunset and the flow of an ordinary river. She wrote about freakish people and she said once that perhaps it took a freak to recognise one.

Does that make me something of a freak? I don't mind, if I could write just a little like Flannery O'Connor.

The veranda was the place for it all

Sydney Morning Herald, 17 October 1985

You hardly ever see verandas these days. You remember them? They ran three parts of the way around houses, in some cases all the way round.

I saw one of these old-fashioned houses the other day being updated. The front veranda was hanging on but about to go. In the meantime it was being used to park the car. The nose of the car nudged the front doorway. It must have been just possible to squeeze past when the people left the house to go to work. While they were away, the man and the woman (no children because one salary paid off the car and the other the renovations), the workmen went on with the building. The front door was always closed.

Decades ago when the house was new the door would have stood open nearly all the time. People passing by would have seen the shiny linoleum on the floor of the hallway and right to the back veranda where the iceman would leave the block of ice.

There would have been children begging splinters to suck, offering them to children hanging over the neighbouring fence. There were no reprimands for this abuse of hygiene. Better an exchange of love at the risk of a few germs.

When there was an outbreak of measles there was sometimes the quaint practice of well children sleeping with the sick ones to contact the disease and "get it over and done with". They crossed one veranda and went to another to observe this ritual, for this was often where the children slept.

They all got better fairly quickly, mostly without complications, and who wouldn't, waking to the sun tickling

spotted faces and the carolling of magpies from the telephone wires.

Clothes were dried on those verandas. The corners
were the best place for lines, because they caught the
breeze coming and going. The napkins flapped whitely
there and people passing felt good at the sight. The little
new one was evidently weeing and doing the other with
healthy regularity. The little nighties, puffed out with the
wind looking eager to be dry and back on baby's body
again.

Soon the baby would be out there on the veranda in the
bassinette under a mosquito net. Here was a real treat for
the passers-by, especially when the babe was done with
sleeping and the arms no thicker than pipe stems could be
seen waving back and forth, back and forth, rather like
human windscreen wipers. But people would have
laughed at that comparison. And with the air so clean and
pure there would be nothing for the little hands to clear
away.

This house I saw was getting a top floor. If there were
to be children they would have to look out on the world
from there, something forbidden when the house was
young. To hang from a window was a breach of etiquette,
even to peep through a slit between curtain and the edge
of the window earned a reprimand.

No, the veranda was the place for it all. To watch for
the postman, to hold out the billy can for the milkman, to
take the bread from the baker. Seldom did visitors need to
rap on a closed door. They were mostly crushed near to
death with embraces and deafened by the welcoming
committee there on the veranda.

I wonder what those long-ago housewives would have
thought of a great crouching metal and chrome motor
car, marking their nice clean boards with ugly black tyres.

Probably chased it off with their brooms.

Tea time's humbling moment

Sydney Morning Herald, 14 February 1985

There is a little stack of cups without handles in one of my cupboards. I should throw them out, at least all except one, kept for measuring cooking ingredients like flour and sugar.

They were never discarded back between the mid-twenties and thirties when the Great Depression crept over the land and hung about like an unwanted guest, then did eventually leave, disappearing gradually (like a guest finally taking the hint) so that the shape appeared like a mirage and those looking hard and long saw it even after it was gone.

There were a lot of cups without handles in those years. Poly cups they were called. Or just polies.

Our table at home for eight children and our parents was set with the cups in one corner. Heaven knows why, but that was the style of our table setting, the cups and saucers solid white with a thin gold line for trim stretched towards the middle of the table, encroaching on space reserved for other foods. This had the effect of detracting from the absence of other foods when times were really bad.

The spoons were set in the saucers in line with the cup handle where there was one. There was much tipping of the head to one side by the table setter to get the angle right with only two little stubs for guidance in the case of the poly.

For there was always at least one poly. It was a major disaster in our household if a cup was dropped and smashed by one whiningly wiping up, and it was a serious enough offence when a handle was wrenched off pushing the teatowel through it with hands that wanted to be doing something else.

When this happened it became a poly and was set out with the others and someone had to have it.

It was fairest to take turns. "Whose turn is it for the poly?" someone would ask, and no one would lay claim to the honour.

It could be a humiliating experience — manipulating the poly full of hot tea, opposite a sister delicately sipping with a little finger curled, setting the cup down with a re-fined little clink of china, winning approving glances from the parents, strong on good manners at the table, while you all but dropped your load, burning your hands raw hanging on and getting a generous splashing down your front as you slurped at the contents.

Sometimes a child would begin wandering about the place, communicating with no one, carrying a long stick with which he beat fences, veranda posts and tree trunks. He would shroud himself in an overcoat in the middle of January.

Our father, who had no diploma in child studies, no degree in psychology and who never told us about his schooldays because he had none, would coax a statement from the small sufferer.

He'd been given the poly three days in a row.

The cure was cheap, simple and uncomplicated, in keeping with the times. He was not to have the poly for a week.

Visitors, and no messing

Sydney Morning Herald, 20 February 1986

A practice that went out of style with running boards on cars and telephone earpieces like skipping-rope handles was the ritual of Getting Ready for Visitors.

Regardless of the length of the stay—two hours, two weeks or two years; and whether it was a bachelor uncle who normally ate all his meals from a table spread with newspaper, or cousins who spent most of their lives in boarding school and were unimpressed by starched pillow cases and lavender in the linen cupboard—the preparations seldom varied.

The house was cleaned from end to end, food laid in as if a famine was imminent, the garden weeded and, if there was a dairy and fowl-run, these were given a thorough overhaul as well.

The female adults were usually thrown into a great state of flux. Few households were without a young aunt or big sister in those times, waiting around for Mr Right (or Mr Wrong, who sometimes had to do as time ran out). And since their chances were boosted by evidence of household skills, they fretted along with the lady of the house that they might Never Have the Place Ready in Time.

It was no use for example, scrubbing veranda boards, blackleading stoves and whitewashing fireplaces to have them messed up before the visitors had a chance to see them at their best.

It was hard on the children, too. They had to refuse to join in marbles and hopscotch and looking for tadpoles in the creek. "We're Having Visitors," they explained in sad little voices. A lot of the menial jobs fell to them.

Our mother came home once from a visit long-anticipated, and we children were eager for details. Families were like that in those days. We yearned to know what she was given to eat, what was said, what was worn and most particularly, What The Kids Were Doing.

But she put away the jam and pickles she brought back with a melancholy air and was heard to whisper to an aunt that the paper on the pantry shelf had not been changed since her previous visit, one year ago. "I didn't feel I was that welcome," she mourned.

Things are different today. When mothers telephone they are visiting daughters or daughters-in-law they are asked to lunch (of course) but it is suggested they pick up hamburgers on the way over.

They also have to pick their way through wheel toys, Cabbage Patch dolls, Care Bears, strewn clothes belonging to Barbie dolls, and if there is a chair with space on it for sitting, a child and book is usually dumped on their knee.

The ironing board is on standby with a husband's weekly supply of shirts and extras might include badges to sew on Brownie uniforms and numbers on football jerseys.

No doubt at all about the welcome there.

A new dress? It's hardly worth the wait

Sydney Morning Herald, 7 March 1985

My sister telephoned me in a state of depression about a new iron she bought. No, it did not fail to hiss and puff in the bossy way irons do, or gather up her new silk petticoat and make a little mound of it like a wrinkled toadstool. It was the method of purchase that affected her.

Her old iron was the one she had had for twenty-five

years and when it broke down she doubted there would be parts available for the repairs, which would probably cost nearly as much as a new one.

She was part-way through ironing a shirt for her son when it died, and she gave her son, there in his underpants, $40 to go out and buy a new one.

She remembered buying the old one.

She and her husband had watched the papers for sales, went to retail stores large and small, to every electrical outlet on their side of the Harbour Bridge, and finally found the one suiting their lifestyle and pocket.

"I think I'll hate that new iron every time I use it," my sister said.

I took a similar aversion (though only temporarily) to overseas holidays when visiting other relatives and the wife said she kept forgetting to book a trip to Great Britain and Europe every time she went to the shops.

When she was at home unpacking the bread and potatoes and dog food, she noticed the return air-fare tickets to London plus twenty-seven-day tour of the Continent and seven days on the Greek Islands had not been bought yet again.

I thought about this family when I first knew them. The husband got holidays but they could not afford to go away, even to Terrigal or the Blue Mountains.

They would have a day in the city going around the shops, and another day out to Manly and back on the ferry. They went every year to the Royal Easter Show and spent eleven months and three weeks looking forward to the next one.

Since the husband retired in 1976, they have been to Great Britain and Europe twice, to Hong Kong three times, to Disneyland twice, three times to the Barrier Reef and once to Bali.

But if you want a barometer of the times, a yardstick

by which is measured the length and breadth of the consumer society, there is the case of the $150 silk dress that went out for the paper collection.

When wrapped in its tissue paper it did not look much larger than a man's handkerchief, and the wife, distracted by a telephone call from a friend whose daughter had gone missing, left it there in the shopping basket with more tissue paper, dry-cleaning dockets and unused bags from the supermarket.

When she saw everyone on the block had put their unwanted papers out for collection, she upended the basket on top of the heap in the garage and dragged the lot in a carton to the footpath, pleased she hadn't missed the collection for the third successive time.

She had bought the dress for a dinner with business colleagues of her husband's and their wives, and didn't even recall it when he saw her in her old black and said it was a favourite of his (he had been afraid she might go out and buy a $150 new one).

She only remembered when one of the other wives came into the restaurant in a new dress floating about her figure the way hers had floated, and she shrieked and clapped a hand to her mouth.

At home she sat in deep misery on the bedroom chair, refusing to go to bed. He opened his wallet (a mean man normally) and pulled out a great many twenty-dollar bills, offering them for a replacement dress.

She put a foot up in its elegant shoe and kicked the wallet so that the money fell like a shower of rust-coloured leaves on the carpet. Neither picked them up and they were there next morning to walk through on the way to the bathroom.

Once upon a time . . .

New Parent, April-May 1985

This is no fairy story although it starts off Once Upon A Time. The time was the forties, when the Second World War was dragging to a close. But there was another war rampant in households where there were infant children, and this was extended well beyond the cessation of military hostilities.

On the one side were the mothers fighting their natural instincts to nurse, cuddle, feed and soothe their offspring. On the other was the enemy using every available weapon to have them do the opposite.

The general of the more powerful side was a book called *Our Babies* and a race of Baby Health Centre sisters were Next in Command. They were invariably flat of stomach, narrow of hip, stern of countenance and so virginal to the eye, they made the poor young mothers feel positively wanton, as if they needed first of all to apologise for taking part in the act that eventually brought them to sit babe on knee on the wooden chair on the other side of Sister's desk.

After weighing, looking for cradle cap, frowning on a weeping navel, frowning even more deeply on the quality and quantity of clothing the child wore, the mothers were asked if they had a copy of The Book. They usually did. It was often delivered to the mother in hospital before she had time to ask the sex of her child or its weight. (There were no hand-holding fathers in the delivery room in those days: serious doubts were held on their ability to follow the Book's text, and at no time were they encouraged to change or burp the baby, being regarded as greater nincompoops than the mothers.)

The Book was the doctor's bible too. Should a young

mother, convinced her child was near death through mal-nutrition, worried about his bow legs (The Book always referred to the baby as "he") or certain his eyes were crossed, manage an appointment to sit on the other side of His desk he poised his fingers at once over the bell at his right hand. "Have you a copy of *Our Babies*?" he would ask, with an expression similar to that worn per-manently by the Health Sister. Since the mother was in-variably in possession of same, the doctor would bring his hand down smartly on the bell calling in the next patient.

Oddly mothers-in-law and other close relatives were often keen devotees of The Book. "If only it had been around in my day!" were the sighing words from many a matronly bosom. This bosom had most likely fed when the owner detected a cry of hunger, taken the baby into bed with her all night, and done the housework with one arm, the other clasping the infant to breast, shoulder or waist.

Where the same mother-in-law would once look for faulty execution of domestic duties (like untidy cup-boards, grimy curtains and dust at the edge of the carpet square) she now looked for tell-tale traces of non-obedience to The Book. "You're NOT giving him a dummy, I hope!" was a frequent cry, accompanied by a rustle through the pages to expose an illustration of a dummy (often called a comforter) liberally covered with flies.

Four-hourly feeding, NEVER picking him up when he cried, and weaning him on the dot of nine months of age were rules number one, two and three. "He seems hungry before it's feed time," would be spoken in quavering tones to the Sister. "A teaspoon of cool boiled water then," said the prim mouth under the glittering glasses. What she didn't say was It's there in The Book, you blith-ering idiot. She too would get ready for the next patient, and there would be nothing else to do but wrap the bunny rug more tightly around the wriggling, grunting, unhappy little shape and go down the Health Centre steps.

Of course the boiled water had been offered already scores of times. The little lips would not open to take it, so it was often thrown in when the mouth was open in a roar. Then there was pandemonium, the child would turn scarlet and purple and appear to be choking to death. The mother weeping now as loud as the child would thump and shake him back to life, then peel him of his wet clothes, both snivelling and sobbing, while he was put into fresh ones, then held in deep guilt close to the tight full breasts that were ready to pour forth nourishment and comfort, except that the BOOK said otherwise. "Pick him up when he cries and you will turn him into a demanding little tyrant, ruling the household," was spelled out. "Put him in his cot in his room and close the door and let him cry it out," the instructions continued. So the mothers did, switching the vacuum cleaner off every two minutes to check that the noise was continuing. It always was. It dropped to a feeble, whining bleat, then stopped. Silence followed for a moment, then the screeching started up again. "He will soon tire of his little game, if you don't give in to him, and fall asleep," said The Book. When and if he did stop, through sheer exhaustion, the mother exhausted too would rush to see that he hadn't died. Of course he would open his eyes instantly, turn a woebegone face to her, eyes filling with a new flood of tears. The Book explains those tears. "They are not genuine, merely turned on to fool you into thinking he is in pain."

While mothers were ordered to feed by the clock, they were told just as firmly to wean by the calendar. Many Sisters insisted on it completed at nine months, not started. "Of course you are not feeding him between six p.m. and six a.m., so weaning should produce no problems," said The Book. All the mother had to do was cut out a breast feed every couple of days and by the end of the week the big job was done. No rock hard breasts, no little head flung down to nuzzle around them, no woeful expressions when little hands were dragged away? No fears that the child may fall ill weeks after the weaning was complete and both mother and child yearn desperately for the comfort of a soft pillow of a breast and warm wonderful mother's milk?

When I tell my daughters and daughters-in-law about these times (with their babies fed on demand, cuddled in bed with their parents, and on the breast up to their second birthday) they say in a chorus "But surely you KNEW how wrong it all was!"

Of course a lot of us knew. A lot of us lied and cheated, sneaked the nipple into a little mouth when a little head was hot with a temperature, or a little arm was grazed with a tumble from a dinkie. We fell asleep over the forbidden two a.m. feed and kept the baby warm and snug in the crook of our arm but failed to confess any of this to Sister, mother-in-law or doctor.

We did not all walk around watching the clock hands turn with maddening slowness to the four hourly feed time, to a chorus of shrieking from behind a closed door.

We actually turned the clock face to the wall and shut ourselves behind the closed door to hear with great joy the chuckle of triumph that broke right into an angry shriek, then gulp, gulp, gurgle, gurgle and the last tear running into a crease made by the biggest baby smile ever seen.

There is an Underground Movement in every war.

FORTY YEARS ON FROM THE WAR

The fortieth anniversary of the end of the Second World War stirred many Australians to look back on their role in the war, and to reflect upon the changes which had taken place as a result of those six difficult years. Masters was ticking over on the subject. She was interviewed by the ABC for a fourteen-part radio series entitled "'The Home Front'', and she had occasion in other interviews to comment upon what she saw as the major effects of the war on Australian society. Most importantly, she was busy tapping her own memories of wartime Sydney in order to create the setting for her new novel, **Amy's Children**.

In her interview for ''The Home Front'', Masters touched upon a number of subjects: the feelings which greeted the outbreak of war, the fears of a Japanese invasion in 1942, the impact of American soldiers and wartime work on Australian women, and the dropping of the two atom bombs on Japan. Not surprisingly for Masters, she placed 1939 in the context of the Depression which had led up to it. Remembering the night of 3 September 1939, when Australia declared war on Germany, she said: ''The people were all standing about with their newspapers, shocked. The look on their faces seemed to say, 'What is happening?

What is happening?' You felt like going up to them and talking about the situation. You felt an excitement too, you know. Perhaps it's not a good thing to confess, but all young people feel excitement when major change is about to take place. You forget about the death and destruction. The 1930s had been a grim, slow time for young people.'' Three years later, at the height of the fears of a Japanese invasion, she remembered how she felt as a young mother living at Ettalong on the New South Wales central coast: ''It was a desolate feeling. I walked down to the beach and along the sea front and thought: Will this always belong to us? The boys were small and I thought: If something happens to me, who will rear them? But I do remember seeing the beauty, it's a very nice spot, and thinking what would happen if it didn't belong to us any more—and how likely that was.''

Of most interest to Masters was the impact of war on Australian women. During an interview about **Loving Daughters**, Masters argued that male-female relationships had changed significantly since the late 1920s, and much of this difference was due to the war: ''World War II brought about a change when women struck out and did jobs equal to the men. I think that's when women found their footing in society. They really got out of the kitchen and into the workforce properly . . . the jobs had to be done by somebody and somebody happened to be the women who had loads and loads of talent.'' Although she saw for herself the pressure on women to leave their jobs meekly at the end of the war—''It was accepted that the right thing was to step down and let the boys have their jobs back again''—a blow had nevertheless been struck for the liberation of women. The thousands of Americans who poured into the cities also changed the way Australian women felt about themselves. The brash gallantry and charm, the attentiveness, the large leave allowances:

these were all disarming, to say the least. Masters has a
nice anecdote about crossing Hyde Park with her
younger sister Del:

> Coming towards us was a group of American soldiers,
> very smart, very handsome. They stopped and said to my
> sister, ''Excuse me, but you're beautiful.'' We thought it
> was a joke! To this day I feel embarrassed to think of it. I
> thought he was being funny. I had never heard an Austra-
> lian say to a perfect stranger, ''You're beautiful'' without
> having some ulterior motive in mind. I haven't heard
> them anyway, ulterior motive or not. It was something en-
> tirely different to the Australian way. Australian men just
> didn't talk like that to women. When we brushed them off,
> taking it as a joke, they were quite hurt. They said, ''That's
> typical of Australians, give a compliment and look what
> happens'', and they sort of threw their hands in the air and
> strode on.

The two articles presented here are personal reminiscences about the end of the war, each taking as its
focus one day in particular: VE Day and VJ Day 1945.
The first recreates the austerity of those times, and the
moment of victory in Europe which somehow seemed,
both at the time and in retrospect, to be a moment of little significance. The quiet impassivity of the rural countryside registers Masters' sense of continuing
anticlimax. The second article also probes the notion of
winning. What kind of victory was signalled by the
dropping of two atom bombs on Japan? And on the
domestic front, while wartime work helped some
women to find their feet, for housebound wives and
mothers the war did little but reinforce their sense of dependence and inferiority. For Masters, the dependent
status of women was intimately bound up with the ser-
vility of Australia's colonial posture towards Britain.
Both forms of servitude were soon to change with the
entry of the United States into the war.

VE Day remembered: After forty years there is still no peace

Sydney Morning Herald, 4 May 1985

One day during the first week in May 1945, a voice steadying its emotion opened the news bulletin on the wireless — not called a radio then — with a single sentence.

"Correspondents on the western front agree that the end of the war in Europe is in sight."

I was in the kitchen making biscuits from a wartime recipe: no butter, a little precious sugar, no eggs. You boiled milk and bicarbonate of soda and poured this foaming liquid on dry ingredients, rolled out the dough and cut it into shapes.

With me were my two little boys: Roy, who would be four in October of that year; and Ian, who had turned one the month before.

They were on the floor playing with pots and pans from the one kitchen cupboard. These were mostly of tin, for materials that once made aluminium and enamel goods now made bullets and fighter planes. No one had seen a shining kettle or saucepan in the shops for three or more years.

For a similar reason the boys were not playing with traditional toys. There were no specialised toy shops, and department stores stocked a meagre supply only at Christmas time.

There were some wooden toys about — wheelbarrows and trucks and blocks — mostly made from timber offcuts by fathers and grandfathers with a talent for such skills and a sorrowing heart that a childhood could pass without a small boy experiencing the joys of a train and rails and a magic Meccano set.

Not that wood offcuts were plentiful either. Building

had all but halted and the sight of a timber frame, the skeleton of a new house, was enough to draw sightseers out for weekend walks to stand and marvel and dream.

I had to upset the boys' game by asking for the tray to bake the biscuits on.

You might have expected them to be using it as a base for landing bombers. Perhaps they were still unaffected by the atmosphere of war, or perhaps they chose the reality of their surroundings, for living in a farming community a few kilometres outside Grafton, in northern New South Wales, they called the baking tray a paddock and the raised edge a fence. They had made cows and calves and horses from the dough I had trimmed from the biscuits and had set them up in little groups, asking for a pinch or two of flour to help make little heaps of fodder.

Had these boys been born forty years on, they would have used modelling clay bought in packs from the supermarket shelves and the mother — or just as likely the baby sitter — would have been watching television rather than watching them. A plentiful supply of biscuits neatly packaged would have been at hand, so there would have been no need for all that mixing and kneading and rolling.

But there were no supermarkets in those days. The shops had sturdy wooden counters where the mothers and children kept to their side and the shopkeeper to his. There was not much temptation on the shelves for there were no raisins, rice, coconut or tinned fruit, and tea and butter and sugar could be bought only if there were enough government-issued coupons to cover the purchases.

There were no sweets in sight so there was no slapping and shouting as happens at supermarket checkouts; no screaming and yelling and red faces as goods were snatched from little hands and little bodies were lifted and flung without ceremony into supermarket carts.

When we got our supply of essential goods the boys made houses and garages and dog kennels of the empty cardboard containers and these were part of their games with the kitchen pans.

The news bulletin ended and the biscuits went into the oven and I took the boys to the front veranda to look at the river. We were always doing that. There was the Clarence in a great silvery sweep, unchanged, unaffected by this news. It had always looked peaceful anyway.

Could it be true that the killing, the suffering, the fear and the shortages after six and a half years could be coming to an end?

I was making biscuits again (the same kind in the same place with the same small boys at the same game) a few days later on May 8 when, for no reason I could think of immediately, out of nowhere across the quiet paddocks came the long whistle of the train going southwards. The blast went on and on and, after a while, the bell at the school near the road began to clang and another pealed out, people from a house opposite rushing across the road to set the church bell ringing.

Then cars travelling to Grafton one way and to Ulmarra the other had their horns blowing, the sound flying upwards with the dust. The whole countryside seemed alive with sound.

We went to the veranda again. The cows huddled together. One or two bellowed, but it was not a bellow of victory like the other noise.

"The war is over in Europe," I told the boys.

"The cows are frightened," Roy said.

When we came back inside the quiet was too quiet and I wondered if the trains and the cars and the bells stopping their shouting meant it was all a terrible false alarm.

We switched on the wireless and the sound was taken up from inside it. There was the singing of *Roll out the barrel, we'll have a barrel of fun!* It went on interminably and I told myself not to get too excited, too carried away; it could still be a mistake; the wireless stations were always playing tunes like that.

But the song ended and the announcer's voice came on.

"We repeat: Germany has agreed to an unconditional surrender and the armistice has come into force. The war in Europe is over. God save the King."

The voice wobbled to a stop and another announcer took over. He began to describe the scenes in the streets of Sydney. The people had run out of the shops and joined the pedestrians and the cars had halted and the noise of their horns was deafening and people were putting their faces inside the cars and kissing the occupants and many tumbled out to join hands and dance, causing the trams to stop and the people to spill from them and add their feet to the dancing and their voices to the singing.

"And look at the torn-up paper coming from the office windows!" the announcer cried. *"Just look at it!"* (He was so excited he forgot we couldn't see.) *"Oh, I hope some of my bills have been torn up!"*

I stood the boys on the kitchen table to see through the window a flag raised at a window of the Browns' place, two kilometres off.

"The Browns are saying how pleased they are the war is over," I explained.

There was no wind left to lift the flag and the only time there was a dance of colour was when the Browns were trying to make the pole secure. I knew the boys were greatly disappointed to see it such a limp thing; not billowing out, defying the blue autumn sky with a blue brilliance.

"I can smell the biscuits burning," Roy said.

I suppose that after that I sat on the couch and watched the boys go on with their game. The couch (actually called

a bed settee) was one of the few items of furniture manu-
factured in wartime. It had a spring base, a mattress and
a long plank for a back, which sloped when it was a settee
and swung away when it was a bed. It would be the equiv-
alent of today's luxurious fold-away sofa bed. Such an in-
novation shown to us in the 1940s would have seemed like
something from another world.

Our settee was in the kitchen because the house, never
completed, had no lounge or sitting room; just two bedrooms, a hall and this large unlined room where we
cooked and ate our meals. One end was partitioned off
and there was a bath tub there, an iron one, intended to be
cast off as a water trough for the animals but retained
when bathroom fittings were unobtainable.

One of the local farmers had been building the house
for his son, about to be married, but the son joined the
armed forces and his girl stayed in the city and we never
knew what became of either of them. It was the only
housing available when my husband, a schoolteacher,
was transferred to Grafton.

The boys and I waited a long time for their father to
come home.

There was no telephone to inform us of happenings in
the town but the local radio station broadcast the information that Grafton had gone wild too in celebration and
the children had been let out of school when the bells rang
to herald the peace.

The teachers from the primary and high schools gathered at one of the hotels. A pretty young widow led the
race along the streets, singing and shouting as loud as
anyone, perhaps to cover the ache of loss, for her young
soldier husband had died early in the war in North Africa.

An infants' mistress of fifty-five got drunk for the first
time in her life. "Two down and one to go!" she cried,
every time she lifted her glass. The two were Hitler and

Mussolini — both dead — and the one was Japan. The war was to go on for another few months before that country surrendered. She giggled and giggled like one of her pupils whom she would normally reprimand.

Where have all her children gone?

Did some die in Korea or Vietnam or are some sitting at summit meetings planning strategy, not in the traditional theatres of war but against the invasion of the cults of the 1980s, hard drugs and their associated crimes? For it seems when arms of one kind are laid down, others are taken up; the end result the same, the slaughter of our young.

Where, for that matter, has Victory gone?

Perhaps its term was as short as the time it took for a train whistle to blow itself out passing a few farms, for a few cars to toot their horns, some bells to clang and the Browns' flag to flutter once, then go still.

War gave women a first taste of liberation

Sydney Morning Herald, 13 August 1985

I remember nothing of VJ Day, absolutely nothing. Not the hour I heard the news, not the kind of day it was, not the task I was engaged in, nothing of that day.

Perhaps one of the children was sick, upsetting the domestic routine, something contributing to a lapse of memory. I strain my ears for the shouting from the wireless, the blast of car horns, train whistles, for all these must have heralded the end of the war, the real end and not the other, three months earlier on VE Day when the peace treaty was signed in Europe.

But I can't remember anything about it.

Postcard of Cobargo, NSW, in the 1920s. Cobargo is the setting of many of Masters' stories of small town life. It is also the place where she began her career in journalism, joining the local paper, the *Cobargo Chronicle*, as a teenage cadet. (Courtesy Mitchell Library, State Library of New South Wales)

The School of Arts, Cobargo, NSW. It was here, as a young child, that Olga Masters learned an unforgettable lesson about life. Her article on Cobargo, ''Things I'd love to do before I die'', was the first piece of journalism she wrote for the *Sydney Morning Herald*. (Photograph by Julie Lewis)

May Gibbs' illustration for the front cover of a government handbook for mothers, *Our Babies,* April 1941. Masters takes her revenge on this didactic tract in her article on child rearing in the 1940s, "Once upon a time . . .". (Illustration © the Spastic Centre of NSW and the NSW Society for Crippled Children, reprinted by permission of Curtis Brown (Australia) Pty Ltd)

Beauty contests, engagement columns, social news and gossip — a typical women's section page from the *Northern Star*, Lismore, October 1962, with (above) the masthead. Masters worked for this newspaper from the mid-1950s until the mid-1960s. (Courtesy the *Northern Star*)

The masthead and "Women's News" page from the *St. George and Sutherland Shire Leader* in February 1968. Olga Masters worked on this women's section in the late 1960s. (Courtesy the *Leader*)

The *Land*'s "Woman's Interest" page with (inset) the front page of 20 March 1969, showing the paper's rural interests. Masters joined the staff in 1969. (Courtesy the *Land*)

Exclusive

Manly's Florist

MARGARET ANNE
1 Sydney Road, Manly
Deliveries Everywhere
977 3287 977 3561
A.H. 969 4032

The Manly Daily

99,000 READERS DAILY

26 Sydney Road, Manly, 2095

977 3333 (15 lines). Night Ads. 977 3246.

Vol. 67. No. 16,120.

SATURDAY, JUNE 22, 1974

PRICE 5c

DRY AND COLD
6-16 Degrees

Mummulgum's proudest mum goes to the Manly match...

— and she took along a batch of rock cakes

(NOT FOR THROWING AT THE EAGLES)

By
OLGA MASTERS
Daily social writer.

All the male reporters were down with 'flu Thursday and there was a threat that no one would be available to report the Manly-Penrith match at Brookvale Oval.

Late in the afternoon the Editor suggested I go along.

This come in a great surprise, because I did not know anyone in the office was aware of my affiliation with the Rugby League through my boy Roy.

Wisely I keep my personal life to myself, and never mentioned that my boy Roy took the infamous Australian schoolboy Rugby League team to England in 1972 and his brilliant coaching resulted in their line being crossed only once in the 13-match tour.

He came back to take a national coaching examination with a distinction, and joined the Penrith club as a coach for the premiership 1974 season.

When told of my assignment I flew to the phone to make yet another illegal call to Penrith.

Roy told me not to worry; he would fill me in on the game and explain each quaint phrases like scrum going down, finding touch, and so on.

In fact he said he could tell me the score then.

"With Ashurst kicking, Stephenson getting most of the ball, Glen West running like a deer, Walker taking every goal, we should be jake."

"We should be level at the half time," said my boy Roy.

"The last two points in the last five minutes of play could go either way. Probably ours."

I went home and baked a batch of rock cakes for boys to share with the team on their ride home to Penrith after the match.

Blue eyes

I took the tin to him in the coach's box at the start of the game.

This was a disappointment. I thought he would be in his blue coach's gear — a perfect match for his eyes — but he was in an orange-coloured shirt, tweed sports coat and brown pants, and looked an ordinary person.

I went and sat close to the oval and my thoughts went back over the years to the days when he was in his six-stone team at Mummulgum.

Then a thought hit me. Oranges! Where were the oranges?

At Mummulgum we mothers used to go on after the game with oranges cut into quarters and handed them out for the players to suck to ease their parched throats.

I left the ground and took a mile along Pittwater Road to find a fruit shop. There were people inside with glazed eyes, and fool-

loneliness, he must have flayed the air with his great arms and accidently hit someone.

I turned back dumbly so he could cut them into quarters, like we did in Mummulgum.

But my boy Roy, as well as everything also, was in Queen's Scout in his youth and he always carried his six-bladed knife, adding in recent years a corkscrew — through association with some of the rougher types — and table unfortunately, in the process of reaching adulthood.

I raced to the coach's box.

I asked for the loan of his knife.

"Don't Mum, don't!" he cried.

"Don't cut your throat until the game is over."

One moment forward to serve me, like he was in a trance.

"Hamilton is back in form . . . Eadie is brilliant . . . there's no holding them now . . . we'll make it to the finals."

These names were unfamiliar to me, so they must have following another code of football perhaps the World Cup Soccer series — as they were New Australians.

I ran back to the ground with my oranges.

An interested bystander looked at me counting them out on the seat.

"You won't need one for Ashurst, lady," he said, "He's been sent off!"

Darling

I wheeled round and looked for my Big Bill, who only a couple of weeks ago had cooked a steak for me at a Penrith barbecue.

I could not see his amiable lumbering figure and his darling black head.

"Why, oh why?" cried.

"Rough play, luv." He wouldn't have meant it.

Out there on that cold, bleak field he would have been homesick for the chaffinch singing in the orchard bough in England now and, in passion of the

Her boy Roy . . . from the family album.

ish grins on their faces, and the one with a radio going full blast.

One moved forward to serve me, like he was in a trance.

Passionate

I went back to my place and naturally had to have my back to the field to cut up the oranges.

But I kept my ear on the game, as it were, through the spectators around me.

I knew we must have been winning because they were all Manly supporters and were yelling. "Kill the bastards."

These are the kind of things said at the height of a passionate desire to see Manly win — an understandable attitude, with opposition like Penrith.

I put the cut-up oranges back into the bag to take them to Roy.

I raced after him into the dressing shed because it appeared that, as the players were coming off, the game was over.

Someone rudely tried to shut the door in my face.

"Get out, lady," said that large burly man. "They're changing."

This was ridiculous.

My boy Roy was in there and I had seen him without his clothes hundreds of times.

Besides, I had to ask him which side took the last two points.

● Manly coach, Ron Willey, tells it his way on the back page.

Big Bill . . . from the field of play.

10 years jail for The Cat

The Newport cat burglar was sentenced to 10 years' jail in the District Criminal Court yesterday.

He is Helmut Ernest Kalt, 21, of Newport and Port Macquarie.

Judge Melville fixed a non-parole period at 21 years, noting that many of the offences had been committed while Kalt was on parole.

Referring to a previous warning to Kalt, who is Austrian-born, about deportation, the judge directed the papers in the case be forwarded to the Department of Immigration.

He also directed that the sentence commence from yesterday.

Kalt was arrested on February 18 last.

Kalt had pleaded guilty in Manly Court on March 13 to nine charges of breaking, entering and stealing.

He asked Judge Melville to take into account 121 other offences.

Judge Melville said the value of property stolen was $167,000, of which $36,000 had not been recovered and identified.

A further $15,000 worth had been recovered, but not identified.

Judge Melville said the nine charges referred to robberies between November 25, 1972, and January 1974, and the other 121 offences from the period August 6, 1972, to January 25 last.

"It was sought to cast some glamour on your detective, and that you were a cool and cute cat-burglar, a gentlemanly fashion.

"Much was made of your physical fitness and your early morning runs on our own beaches.

"Much of what was said in mitigation of your offences was mundane nonsense."

(Mr Bruce Miles, solicitor, appeared for Kalt at the hearing on June 3 last.)

He said Kalt had been employed by a Mr Blossom in Manly and Port Macquarie.

"This was to mask your offences which were carried out for your personal advancement.

"You may be said to have engaged in the business of an habitual criminal."

His Honour added that a psychiatrist had reported no psychological disturbance in Kalt and had said he should be dealt with on the legal merits of the case.

Judge Melville said Kalt's approach to normal behaviour was almost completely lacking, adding that further action might be taken against him because of parole breaches.

SAVE
UP TO
$600
ON OUR COMPANY DEMONSTRATORS
NOW!

Dial a Deal Right Away on
948 0281

WHITE LEYLAND
449 SYDNEY RD., BALGOWLAH

Olga Masters was a senior journalist with the *Manly Daily* from 1971 until 1983. "My Boy Roy", published in June 1974, is still remembered today as one of her best feature articles.
(Courtesy *Manly Daily*)

This cartoon illustration appeared at the top of Masters' popular "Style" columns for the *Sydney Morning Herald* from 1984 to 1986. (Courtesy *Sydney Morning Herald*)

Claude Monet, *The Meadow* (c. 1879). When Masters saw this painting on exhibition in Sydney in 1985, she was prompted to write of her feeling of kinship with the French Impressionist painter. (Reprinted, by permission, from Collection, Joslyn Art Museum, Omaha, Nebraska, gift of Mr William Averell Harriman)

Olga Masters in Tashkent, Russia, with travelling companions Tom Shapcott (left) and Chris Wallace-Crabbe (right). The three Australian writers were on a tour of Russia jointly sponsored by the Literature Board of the Australia Council and the Soviet Writers' Union, October–November 1985. (Courtesy the Australia Council)

In Moscow, at the office of the magazine *Soviet Literature* (from left to right) Anna Martinova (head of International Programs), Eugeny Krivitsky (assistant head in chief), Tom Shapcott, Olga Masters, Chris Wallace-Crabbe. Martinova's curiosity about the status of women's writing in Australia, and her concern to see more Soviet women in print, impressed Masters. (Courtesy the Australia Council)

A shameful confession that, particularly with the memory of VE Day remaining so clear after forty years.

One reason might be the tie with the Mother Country, as England was called then, that gave so much significance to Victory in Europe. We were conditioned to revere her. She was more than the Mother Country—she was the Mother under whose skirts we had sheltered for more than one hundred years, on whom we depended. We always knew she would put things right in the end.

Perhaps VJ Day came as a sort of anticlimax. The Bomb was dropped and that was an ending of a kind. We had won. Winning has always been of great importance.

We were, of course, deeply frightened when Japan came into the war. The bombing of Pearl Harbour was terrifying news. We listened to the wireless through the fall of Singapore and while the enemy inched its way down New Guinea—not too far away as it happened, living as we were then on the mid North Coast of New South Wales.

But the fears were in bursts, rippling across the surface of our lives, young mothers with children, meals to find from fairly flat purses and well-handled ration books.

A neighbour would come in with a child on her hip to talk about what we would do if the Japs came.

One or another had relatives in a remote part of the continent offering to take her in. Another was thinking of an air-raid shelter in the backyard, but it seemed a shame to tear up the garden after all the hard work.

We were not told of the air-raid on Darwin until the event was more than a week old. We were rather like children with the birth of a sibling kept from us until all dangers had passed and father could announce all was well.

Japanese submarines came into Sydney Harbour but we chased them off. They might have been small boys throwing stones at our high, well-barred windows. We might have said, "Phew, that was close".

We were a pretty naive lot in those days. Not only did we still believe if God saved the King he would save us too, we did most of the things our mothers did and their mothers before them, and nearly all of them came from the United Kingdom, the very name suggesting power, protection and obedience. Our obedience.

We inherited from our forebears the idea that women were inferior to men and here, by George, it was being proved. They were over there and up there fighting for our land and our lives, regardless of the safety of their own. If flat feet or curvature of the spine kept them out of the forces, they were working in an essential industry.

Our job was to brush the hearth, see that dinner was ready on time, and vote the way they told us to.

Not only were we naive by today's standards, but downright ignorant. Jogging was something we did when the butcher was selling sausages without asking for meat coupons. Heroin would have sounded like the name of a bird. We never knew of a child dying of cancer. The pill was taken for constipation. Gay was the way we felt most of the time, even while twenty-two thousand Australian men and women were prisoners of the Japanese.

We had tennis on Wednesdays, and if the conversation got around to marital relations, the word sex was not used. It was heard only when our children were born and we wanted to know if they were boy or girl.

It is true that war shapes our lives. Perhaps truer to say it reshapes them. Truer perhaps of women than men.

The American servicemen had something to do with the reshaping. They opened car doors, brought flowers, told the women they were beautiful, talked to the married ones with children as well as the young and single. They sent home to the US for the first silk stockings we had seen in years. Perhaps they listened more attentively than the Australian men. Whatever it was, some time during those years and afterwards a confidence grew, a belief in the person one was.

Not every woman holding down a man's job while he was at the front gave it up when he returned without some forceful speaking (this was considered an attitude of the most unladylike kind). Some time later — it took up to twenty years — came the creeping revolution and there was almost a full-scale entry into what was quaintly called a man's domain and women got a voice in running the country — with and without a war — and made it known they weren't just there to see to the supper.

There was something else we did with equal thoroughness during the war.

We hated. We hated the Japanese — not only the leaders of the war, the instigators of the slaughter, deprivation and suffering, but every one — born and unborn.

When Pearl Harbour was bombed a woman in a Sydney department store smashed down a stand of china stamped "Made in Japan". A shop assistant came up with a dustpan and swept the pieces into a bin. His face was as grim as hers. He could not, at the risk of losing his job, have done such a thing, but he was glad somebody did.

Last month in Western Australia I watched while nine thousand American sailors poured off nuclear warships for rest and recreation leave after months in the Indian Ocean.

The clock might have been turned back forty years. Outside the port, there was the rush to join the queue for taxis, the flash of shiny black shoes, sailor collars lifted in the wind, duffle bags dumped on the footpath. Heads were lifted to sniff air no longer pungent with salt. New smells. A perfumed shrub, smoke from a wood fire, fumes from cars and buses, a tarred road, the scent from a woman's ears and wrists.

There were little knots of the women, with backs half-turned, as if meeting a sailor was the last thing they had in mind.

Under the white, gobs' caps, the clean shaven faces, the short cropped hair, the sailors were no different to the servicemen of the forties.

But some were Japanese.

AROUND THE HOUSE

Many of Olga Masters' columns celebrate disorderliness of an old-fashioned and familiar kind, where housekeeping is a misnomer and where **Home Beautiful** standards of perfection only ever exist in the houses of others. For Masters, "home" is peopled by speaking objects. Ugly, unwanted presents demand to be on full view, and the fancy new dishwasher can never prevail over the sink because it obliterates the narrative possibilities of a used teacup.

Some things you never miss until you move

Sydney Morning Herald, 17 January 1985

Once when we moved house we found a power point we didn't know was there. There was great excitement when it was discovered on a skirting board behind a bed, and several pairs of hands slapped the dust away and half a dozen voices cried as one: "Look at THAT."

The occupier of the bed said he could have plugged a radio in and had his own bed lamp. He stopped in the packing and huddled in a heap staring at the three little points, dreaming of what he had missed.

That is the way with moving. You discover all you have missed.

And dust the skirting boards for the first time since the previous owner dusted them for you to move in.

After that you go around the picture rails, which suffered a similar affliction, and more little jobs come up and as you do them your attachment to the house grows deeper and deeper.

Outside, the husband moves a heap of old palings and broken flower pots, and a quaint little nook is discovered with which the wife could have done wonders.

These things do not escape the new owners.

"Look, Jake," she cries. "We can grow an antigonon leptopis in that corner." (The people who buy our houses always give shrubs their botanical names.)

They always wear the right clothes for buying houses too, beautifully creased slacks, not like us who snatch things from the clothesline and jump into them to get in the car and go and look at the houses we buy.

They come frequently and unexpectedly to measure between walls and doors to see if their wardrobes will fit, and because one of their revolting children has reported groans and creaks when he jumped on some of the floorboards.

They come at mealtime and cry out their well-rehearsed apologies that they will go and sit in the car until we're finished, and we think depressingly of their matching china washed and put away in their tidy kitchen, for the people who buy our houses always live normally right up to the minute the pantechnicon backs up their driveway.

They are the kind who never use old coffee cups for tooth glasses but ones of fine porcelain made in Italy; who never have mistakes with their washing and everything comes out green or pink or a deep donkey brown,

and moaning, complaining husbands and children who
have to wear them until ten washes later when they are
back to normal.

The more they come to the house the more we learn
about them, and the more we love our house and do not
want them to have it.

But we make the last trip to the new place finally, and
Christopher, the whimsical, thoughtful one is the first to
speak.

"In the new house we should each have a job looking
after something," he said.

Roy said he might do something if he could spare the
time from football.

"Someone should dust the skirting boards," Deb said.
"But not me."

The other day I pulled out a bookcase and saw behind
it. Then all along the rest of the skirting boards.

There were miles of them, and miles of picture rails, all
bearing this dark brown fuzzy line, like an army of soldiers on the edge of a cliff, contemplating mass suicide.

My husband asked if I was contemplating a massive
clean-up.

But I said no, I was thinking of moving.

Here's a friendly hint for Sunday —
stay in bed

Sydney Morning Herald, 19 December 1985

More than a few people have their Sundays ruined by The
Hints. For some unexplained reason, given that Sunday is
a day of rest, newspapers serve up a column or two of
them under headings like Handy Hints, Star Hints, Take
a Hint.

Hint, Hint would be appropriate since they act like a dig in the ribs to those slothful creatures who gather the papers from the front lawn and crawl back to bed with them staying there until the sinful hour of ten o'clock.

They could doze off before they reach The Hints but seldom do. In fact, there is a magnetism about those columns that bring on a state of paranoia over neglected areas of the housekeeping and urge the body to rush to kitchen, bathroom, garden, even the garage, to make amends.

But imagine the effect on the rest of the family if this happened. Imagine me for example calling out: Charles, Roy, Ian, Quentin, Chris, Sue, Deb, Michael! I've just made buckets of lovely hot tea. Then when they appear tell them the tea is to be strained and used for cleaning the windows.

Hints editors appear to have a penchant for tea. They recommend its use for reviving an ailing maidenhair fern and claim it will do a similar job on underwear long past its prime.

Can you imagine the roars from the family stumbling into the bathroom to prepare for football or the beach to find the hand basin filled with old petticoats and pants bubbling out of this brownish mess speckled with leaves that escaped the straining process?

Or the bath filled with plastic food storers, their fancy names of Square Rounds and Wonderliers no longer suiting their browning, greasy and grime-coated state.

Soak your plastic containers in a bath of water with bleach added. Rinse well (obviously to avoid a bulk booking at the undertakers). They will come up like hell they will. That's another thing about The Hints. All those promises. A saucer of ammonia left in the oven overnight will restore the saucer to its original state.

Bring the garden spade inside and be prepared to spend

the next twenty-four hours chipping away at the baked-on grease. The editor must have put his blue pencil through lines like that.

People do not readily confess to reading The Hints. Embarrassed by the fact that my obsession with them caused me to read them before stories on Star Wars and Paul Keating, I was not brave enough to buy a book called *The Best 500 Household Hints in Alphabetical Order*.

I set myself the task of reading a page every time I was in the newsagents. I only reached E (Epsom salts are great for indoor plants, making them green and lush) before the newsagent began clicking his tongue and fiddling with the magazines and stuff nearby and I felt obliged to slink away.

Hints were a great topic of conversation back in those days when women gathered for afternoon tea. Such meetings are out of date now with women in executive jobs, carrying smart briefcases and claiming to Never Touch Cake.

"What delicious lemon cheese!" someone would cry with a mouthful of tart.

"Warm a lemon in the oven and you get twice the amount of juice!" someone would be bound to shout back.

The chocolate cake is praised and Mary confesses that the sour milk is the secret ingredient. Before another crumb is dropped someone else rushes in with the information that a dash of vinegar in fresh milk turns it sour in the time it takes to grease the cake pan.

But if people don't talk about Hints any more they certainly think about them.

Everyone worth their season ticket to the opera suffers distress at the sight of the leading lady trailing her silk gown across the dusty stage and worries far into the night trying to recall what Hint will restore the hemline to its former immaculate state. If they remember they may need a restraining hand to stop them rushing back stage to tell the manager.

Matilda takes the fun out of washing up

Sydney Morning Herald, 18 July 1985

Kitchen sinks are hardly likely to make a comeback. More's the pity. They have been upstaged by that electronic monster, the dishwasher, often given a pet name by the household like Matilda, Florrie, Bess, Jess or Martha.

It does its work with more speed and efficiency than the human counterpart, but none so far have been found to offer a nice soothing cup of tea and a promise that things will be better tomorrow.

Sinks haven't moved out, they just look different now, clinically clean so as not to disgrace the new boss just moved in. There they sit weeping light little tears like an elderly relative knowing they will be packed off to a nursing home when they finally become obsolete.

You never see garden cuttings dumped in them, leaves stuck to their sides, a trickle of earth-coloured water running into the plug hole. Or a scraped dish of rice custard someone found in the refrigerator and ate at the disgraceful hour of 11 p.m.

Gone are such homely touches.

"Have a cup of tea!" the lady of the house would cry to the unexpected visitor.

"But you've just had one!" the visitor cries back. For there in the sink lying on its side on the saucer is a cup dribbling little tan-coloured drops.

There is no law of etiquette forbidding you to look into

sinks. (But you would never have the cheek to open the dishwasher door to peer among the trays to see what this lot has been up to.)

The sink used to control the dinner party. Guests worried about the growing pile of used plates and the cauliflower cheese dish needing attention before the dried edges settled there permanently.

There was usually the cry of "Let's wash up for Mary!" particularly when sparks began to fly from a political conversation which Mary forbade her husband to allow before the couples arrived. The men go with the women to the kitchen and take up teatowels and the anti-Hawkes and pro-Hawkes forget their differences in a study of the shelves Bill made from timber offcuts and there, in Mary's warm and rather cluttered kitchen, they begin to itch for a hammer and saw and get stuck into a similar project at their place.

Youngsters used to grow up around the kitchen sink: Whose turn to wash up tonight? I'll give you twenty cents if you do it and I can save my nails for the dance.

Sometimes the job was raced through, an ear for the roar of a motorbike taking a fifteen-year-old for his first glorious spin around the block in the half-dark of a balmy summer night.

He makes it in time, the sink comes up smiling after the last saucepan. It might say, Well done, enjoy the ride and take care!

Not so the dishwasher. It would probably set up a whine, followed by a guttural mutter.

And stub your toe on the way out.

A home to call your own, salad bowls, vases and all

Sydney Morning Herald, 1 May 1986

The other day I overheard someone make an observation. This person, past middle age, wondered what her house would look like if everything in it was of her own choosing.

You could see she had been through it all. Starting with the wedding presents. The two of them in the halcyon days of their courtship (whatever happened to words like halcyon and courtship?) buying the striped blue and white china they loved. He pictured her roast dinner on the plates, she imagined the tenderness with which he wiped the cups and saucers and stacked them away.

They probably still have the set stacked away. For along comes a sturdy flowered brown-and-fawn job (she hates flowers on china, he hates brown and fawn) which they feel compelled to use since the giver is one of their most frequent callers. It is no accident that the giver's eyes dart from table to dish drainer when she steps into the kitchen.

In fact, so many eyes seem to ask "where is it?" as they trail around the rooms, the couple dare not relegate even the most despised vase or ornament to a dark cupboard.

But things are different now, you are probably saying. Lists are made of needs, and names go beside them as they are met. For example: Toaster—Uncle Herb and Auntie May. Unfortunately Herb and May buy the kind fashionable in their day—a finger-burning contraption that has to be nursed along to avoid it smoking. Relegating it to a dark cupboard would be akin to doing the same to dear old Herb and May.

Even Washing Machine—Mum and Dad, isn't a winner. "We'll get a basic one, nothing fancy, to spare them paying out too much," says bride to groom. (It is her Mum and Dad.)

Things should get easier with relatives dying off and moving away, friendships disintegrating, and so on. There should finally come an end to the mad rush to bring out the punch set, salad bowls and dessert spoons in their fraying velvet-lined boxes when visitors call.

Then the wife may feel free to cry "Let's refurnish! Let's have everything just the way we want it!" (No wiser than when she was a bride.)

For obstruction is closer than they think. Along comes daughter, heavily into health and nutrition, armed with clay cookware and orders to throw away the aluminium baking pan and dripping can that have been the backdrop to roast beef and Yorkshire pudding for forty years. His face and heart drop at the thought of having eaten his last fat-anointed baked potato and thick rich gravy.

"Never mind!" she says "Read the lovely card."

There is a place for that. With all the others treasured since the wedding day, the terribly corny verses wishing them long life and happiness, and crosses for kisses adding to the messages of love.

Who wants a home they can really call their own, anyway?

The truth about keeping house

Sydney Morning Herald, 22 May 1986

Hardly a woman over the age of fifteen hasn't at some stage in her life been inspired by the reams of writing in books and magazines on the subject of keeping house.

It is clearly spelled out that if you have a pair of strong

arms, and legs in a similar state, and a mentality halfway to average, you can have a clean and orderly home and keep within a budget.

You can have filling and nourishing meals on the table and whip up more at a minute's notice, out of a supply of tins and packets kept on a shelf for this very purpose.

It takes years, sometimes a succession of husbands, and a great many children — your own and other people's — to come to terms with the truth.

The very name housekeeping or keeping house is a grave misnomer. You don't keep house at all. You keep what's in it.

The only housekeeping that comes anywhere near the guidelines of the homemakers' journals is on television. Here you see a woman with a spray-can, searching out a non-existent fly in a room so sterile that no self-respecting insect would venture near it.

Since shopping is the master card in the good housekeeper's pack, she needs to be armed with a shopping list made up from a planned week's menus before she steps inside the supermarket door. Very often this is missing, posted with the letters or back at home on the kitchen table.

Everyone knows the only foolproof shopping list is in the next trolley at the checkout. In this there is the brown sugar, the walnuts and the lightbulbs overlooked, and since you are trapped in a queue of a dozen or more, the only alternative is to buy these items at the milk bar on the way home, commonly known as Rookery Nook.

There are other just as reliable methods of wrecking the budget.

Take the last twenty-four hours before the next payday when your purse is as flat as an alley cat's stomach. You decide to take a two-kilometre walk to a cheap butcher and make a stew for dinner. Before you can get outside the door with your string bag cries come from all parts of the house: Take my pen for a refill! Don't forget the dry cleaning! We're out of shampoo!

Keeping house should be dead easy. But first remove the people from it.

The model of a mother

Sydney Morning Herald, 5 December 1985

A woman can go for years and years without a personality change. She can take care of her family, make a great Madeira cake, and control herself admirably at the junior soccer matches on a Saturday morning.

She can be happy with her lot, keep her old, above-ground swimming pool while the neighbours put in kidney shapes and cabanas (and be amused at how little use the cabanas get).

I'm me and happy to be me, she will sing while she does the washing up in a single bowl and sees through the window the delivery of a new dishwasher to next door.

But put her in someone else's house and all this can change. Send her away for a little break from the family with her sister or best friend and there is the risk of this mild-mannered, secure, adjusted lady doing a complete turnabout.

All the wiping-down starts it. The sister wipes down a lot, inside the sink and the draining part, then on to the window sill, the cupboard fronts and over to the fridge.

"You could wipe down forever, I know," she says as if she were an old hand.

She likes looking inside her sister's fridge for the pleasure of seeing the cheeses in their see-through container, without any smudges on the outside, the milk and skim milk and cream grouped together, and the beautifully tight plastic film over basins of leftover rice and potato salad. There is a bowl of prunes that fascinate her like fat black slugs in brown syrup. She would like a couple but she may not be able to get the cover back properly.

She succumbs and eats two, then doesn't know what to do with the stones. As you would guess, there is nothing but a dead match on the bottom of the kitchen tidy, lined with plastic whiter than the brand she buys. There is no hole in the gauze fly screen to poke them through, and her sister polishes the leaves of the indoor plants daily so would find them there. In the end she wraps them in a piece of paper towelling, trimming the ragged edge she left behind, and puts them in her old carrybag.

At night when she should be blissfully asleep in the spare room, she can't nod off because of the grouped family photographs on the wall and the thought of hers between the scarred covers of bulging albums.

She makes resolutions for a Change in Things when she gets home. She will put away the groceries the minute she gets inside after shopping, not find the new packet of cereal two days later on a window sill near where she was called to look at a pair of lizards. The curtains will be washed, the windows cleaned, the broken gate fixed, the shrubbery tamed. Every time she closes her eyes for sleep she thinks of something else and finally sheds a few tears because Everything Will Be Left To Her As Usual.

She fails to get started, though. When she is home she is clasped so tightly by the children and told how much she was missed she can't get free to go to the kitchen and start Wiping Down.

Not that there would be much room around the sink for Wiping Down. No one had Wiped Up while she was gone.

A dreamy spring walk unwanted

Sydney Morning Herald, 31 October 1985

People walk differently in different seasons. They are brisk in autumn, languid in summer, urgent in winter and dreamy in spring. This is the dreamy time. A lot of walking is done at weekends in family groups along suburban streets, especially those with nice gardens. The walks start off in this dreamy ambling way and everything goes well up to a point. They are drawn from one side of the street to the other by the smell of jasmine in one garden and freesias in another.

"Oh, isn't the spring wonderful?" the woman says and takes the husband's arm. He turns to see if someone is looking, not caring too much for a show of affection in public, and not greatly in favour of weekend spring walks with good programs on television at home.

The woman is hurt and drops back to snap off a piece of climbing geranium or golden heart ivy.

The children race up and ask what is she going to do with them. The husband is not a gardener and the woman observing his hurrying back snorts on it. The snort is not in any way connected to an allergy brought on by some newly-flowering shrub.

The further they go the more the family string out. The children take off their jackets and bring them to the mother to carry. She worries that they will catch cold and now that last season's clothes are fully exposed, worries about their replacement.

As if some sort of mental telepathy has been set up, one of the children turns and asks in a whiney voice (they are tired of looking for ladybirds with different-coloured backs) if they can go and look at the shops.

"We're keeping away from the shops," the mother

calls sharply, and the husband, pretty sure this remark is a reflection on his status as a provider, puts his head down and tries to appear to belong to a different group of walkers.

This is the time for the handymen to be out, which this husband is not. There are pergolas going up, little latticed enclosures for climbing roses and hanging baskets, new rockeries, loads of soil ready to be spread by spades charged with a new life like their owners, garden seats and tables getting a fresh coat of paint. It appears everyone who is not out walking for spring is at home working in its honour.

"Oh, look at that!" moans the wife, stopping at the sight of a husband terracing a slope with railway sleepers.

Her husband is too far away to hear now and he sits on a bank by the roadside to take off a shoe and examine a heel where a blister has formed. He walks very little. He has a hole in the toe of his sock and she leans dejectedly on a fence quite a distance away to appear to have no connection with him and the neglected darning.

"I should get a job," the woman says, still in her moany voice and the children, forgetting that this is said early in every spring, go into a tight little knot with a shared vision of no one to spread them bread and jam after school and long terrible days at home alone when they are sick.

The husband puts his shoe back on and stands up and (mental telepathy at work again) they all turn towards home. The heat has brought clouds and they have to hurry to beat the rain.

The house looks cosy and welcoming and they get inside only slightly damp. The husband is glad he did not get around to putting the heater in the attic and the wife is glad that tinned soup will be alright for tea since the weather has turned quite wintry. Everyone is pleased they are allowed to eat around the television.

The pity is, spring comes when some people are not ready for it.

Life & Home

THE FAMILY

Masters' feminism can be seen in her columns about families, several of which dramatise the way in which Australian culture devalues women. The isolating experience of mothering is explored in "The loneliness of long-distance motherhood" and in "Don't forget, mothers are human beings too". Young mothers suffer professional and personal discrimination, while older mothers prove to be the most vulnerable victims of the disintegration of the family unit. In "Never fear, housewives—he's here", which has affinities with the short story "Brown and Green Giraffes" (**The Rose Fancier**), we see how the identification of women with the home leads not just to an unequal division of labour; it also means that household expenditure is perceived by husbands as personal extravagance while the financing of their own "outside" hobbies and pleasures is left out of account.

Three articles in a lighter vein are included here. All touch upon the frustrations of family life: the selfishness of children, the impossibility of coping with an extended family of in-laws and, finally, the family of in-laws which never quite came into being.

The loneliness of long-distance motherhood

Sydney Morning Herald, 1 August 1985

This is the story of a woman who went to the shops every day, but had nothing to buy. All the children at last had left home. Her husband had gone many years before. That's how she explained it. He's been gone this long time, she said, hoping people would think he was dead, ashamed to say he had left her when the seven children were very young and was never seen again.

First there were all of those to bring up on the pension she was ashamed to apply for, then her son's two when his wife left him, and the little boy of her single daughter.

Many times she had thought it would be good to be by herself at last. She could buy some nice towels, bacon she craved for, and a punnet of strawberries.

But that reminded her too much of the little boy (the last to go when his mother got a boyfriend who allowed him to live with them). "Let me write strawberries on the shopping list, Gran!" he yelled to her once, before they went off to buy gravy beef, margarine and day-old bread at half-price.

She thought it would be good to sleep through the night undisturbed. No getting up at 2 a.m. to noises in the kitchen, and finding strange young people there eating the apple pie that was her pudding for dinner that day.

I know I should go crook, she said to herself, going back to bed. But they must be hungry.

Waking now she can hear the house creak, more frightening than the scream of ambulance and police siren, she used to listen for (and hear), fearful that some of her wild young ones might be the victims.

Forty-five years is a long time to work as a mother.

It started at eighteen, when her first was born and lived

for four months. She had all those others soon afterwards, which helped her forget, people said.

The fools. No mother forgets. No reasoning is sound, no explanation acceptable to the one who gave a life and saw it pulled away. They might as well cut out a slice of her shoulder and breast (where she cradled the child) and say, "There, you can manage without that", while the wound stays raw and stinging and weeping for the rest of her life.

She could go out and work for company and to keep occupied, others say. She can cook and clean. But her cooking is old-fashioned now, thick stews with suet dumplings and rice puddings. She never used wring buckets and squeeze mops for her cleaning, but knelt on the floor, scrubbing a square at a time, wiping it dry with an old singlet of her husband's, left behind in his hurry to get away.

What can you do, Madam? She would be too shy to say she could love. That was a four-letter word that was an embarrassment to her generation, used far less freely than that other four-letter word of today.

You have seen her. She wears an unfashionable dress and a cardigan, that rides up at the back and peaks deeply at each corner in front.

She carries a slack old shopping bag, with two chops (she is ashamed to ask the butcher for one), and a cake of washing soap (after all that soap powder for those piles of T-shirts and jeans).

She does not look well. Of course, she isn't. She is suffering a disease called Loneliness. The Loneliness of a Long-Distance Mother. There is no known cure.

Don't forget, mothers are human beings too

Sydney Morning Herald, 5 September 1985

If you read every book on child bearing and rearing from any that came out with the First Fleet through Doctor Spock to the new ones like *Making Love After Birth* nowhere will you find it stated that part of a woman's brain comes away with the afterbirth.

But heaven help her if she is thinking of resuming her career, with suitable arrangements made for the care of her child.

She may find herself in a cubicle interviewed for employment, keeping dark the existence of the child, hoping the subject is not raised. In another may be a man having his hand half wrung off when he announces the recent birth of his child. The interviewer rises in excitement, calling for one of the other bosses whose child was born around the same time.

No question on who the job goes to. He and old Graham will get on like a house on fire. There will be no questions asked either when they compare notes on weight gain, nappy changing, first teeth and smiles that are definitely not wind.

And why does everyone bring hand-knitted bootees for the baby, books by Lady Cilento, a rubber-backed apron for bath time? Why not some lacy, frill-edged panties, since she is now able to see her groin, enrolment in a course on Italian, tickets to a French movie, an adult novel?

She is a social risk if asked out to dinner. She will probably dump the baby basket where it upsets the pleasing decor of the dining room, and as she knows no better, will most likely breastfeed the child several times during the evening, in front of everyone.

One young woman in similar circumstances complained of being addressed only once between arrival and departure.

She was asked how she pegged the napkins out, singly with two pegs to each, or two joined with a single peg. The latter method was quicker if they needed to be brought in hurriedly when rain threatened, and it saved on pegs.

Think about it, dear.

Never fear, housewives — he's here

Sydney Morning Herald, 6 June 1985

You see all those men out there on bowling and golf greens every day of the week? They're fed up with the housework. They couldn't wait to get stuck into it, that and the gardening and shopping.

Every day for forty years, they have witnessed those slovenly, extravagant, time-wasting practices in the home by wives.

Pulling molars, delivering babies, working out the profit on a new shopping complex covering two city blocks, they have itched to be at home giving the brassware its first real clean in forty years, or restoring order to the saucepan cupboard.

They have watched in agony as wives pass over the inserts in newspapers devoted to ways of saving dollars on food, ignoring all that advice on going for the cheaper cuts of meat, soaking them in vinegar and lemon juice and seeing them come up tender enough to be eaten with a spoon.

What do they really see? Time after time a great slab of steak thrown under the griller as they walk in the door.

They know how that steak was bought. "Just give me the dearest cut in the shop, please Butcher," while looking away from the notices pointing out the bargains of the day, specials of the week and lots of give-away prices.

Just give them the shopping bag. They would save enough in six months for a cruise to Noumea.

But it turns out differently.

The wife sets up this banging in the kitchen when she needs the cutting board and it isn't on its end on the bench by the refrigerator where it had stood undisturbed for forty years.

He takes up all the floor rugs to vacuum (properly) and puts them back in the wrong places and even she can't remember where they should go and there is this great sighing and flinging session that lasts half the day.

They don't speak, or she says coldly "Excuse me" or "Do you mind?" when his backside is poking out of the refrigerator as he wipes it out (properly) and she is trying to get past.

Then one day he throws the spade down in the middle of the petunia bed (where there should be perennials to save on all those punnets of seedlings) and goes off in pursuit of a new hobby.

He spends $1,000 on his gear alone.

There is no suggestion that the wife take up bowls or golf. Someone has to do the housework.

The things the kids brought in

Sydney Morning Herald, 3 October 1985

A young friend got a letter from her mother in America. Your father (the mother wrote) has built a shed out the back. The news brought a blush of guilt to the young woman's cheeks.

"It's for our things," the young woman explained. "The chest of drawers I got at an auction, the desk my grandmother left me, my trunk of souvenirs from my trip to Europe, all my ski gear. And my brother's things. He collects motor bike frames and old trumpets."

It happens all the time. The children leave home but their belongings stay. Until their children arrive and you begin a career in baby-sitting. You baby-sit the goods. The same degree of devotion and dedication is required for both.

The goods thin out a little when the new generation emerges. "That big wicker basket of mine," a daughter says. "It will be just the thing for the baby's toys."

The baby at this stage is only a slight bulge under the patchwork overalls with legs at half mast, a great disappointment for her father who was hoping impending motherhood might bring about a less embarrassing and more dignified form of dress.

Cartons of sports pennants, school books, running shoes, postcards from travelling contemporaries and packs of photographs fill the linen cupboard and relegate the pillow slips and table runners to boxes under a bed.

"Surely," mother says to son. "You don't want your old confirmation certificate?"

"No, no!" cries the son in anguished embarrassment for his mates are looking on and they have recently denounced God.

But on the next visit he asks for it. He is making a collage of memorabilia for his flat wall and he wanted it there with his first finger painting and laces from his first football boots.

"But you told me to tear it up!" yells the mother. "I

might have, I might have!" he yells back. "But where have you put the pieces?"

That American mother could have been worse off. Her letter might have read: Dear daughter, Your father has built a shed down the back for us to move into. There is no room in the house.

Handy hints on coping with "the other side"

Sydney Morning Herald, 14 November 1985

All sorts of services are available to couples preparing for marriage, or the alternative, cohabitation. Earnest bodies offer courses in sharing the mortgage, budgeting, bringing up children, and so on. Yet no one appears to offer classes on handling new relatives, keeping foot and mouth apart at weddings and funerals, and who is charged with the responsibility of making the first move to go when visiting.

Some couples celebrate diamond wedding anniversaries before sorting out relationships on what is mostly called "the other side". It ceases to matter then. They have the excuse of loss of memory allied to growing old.

The fact is, sixty years can easily slip by without clarification on which in-law cousins belong to which uncles and aunts, where old Uncle Felix fits in who, in fact, is not a blood relation at all, but a bachelor cobber of the wife's grandfather.

One ventures to say that wives are better at getting the relationships in order. They are often carried away in pre-marriage days with a resolution to love his people like their own and be a model daughter-in-law, slavishly following his mother's recipe for the date scones he adores and the shine on his collar he cannot live without.

The man gets by with nods and grunts, and an occasional smile, believing the whole mob of them can be put to one side like the unsuitable presents when the wedding is over.

But in no time at all he is asking after the health of people whose funeral he was dragged to the year before, confusing the mother of the bride with the sister she hasn't spoken to for twenty years, and complimenting a youngster he takes for the musical prodigy in the family but who, in fact, knows the playing position of every rugby league footballer in the Sydney premiership competition, and nothing else.

Husbands are known to set off to the wrong suburb when visiting, then, when the mistake is discovered, he must endure the wife's aggrieved silence until they arrive. When he stands up to go, she announces she will go around the garden with Maud and collect the promised cuttings. He resolves that next time they are visiting his Auntie Flo, right on cue when she gathers up the children to go, he will look for the five hundredth time in his life at the collection of Uncle Gus's firearms.

Now if there were classes dealing with this sort of thing, everyone would get off to a better start. Just as it is established that the wife's parents pay for the wedding reception, and the groom has certain financial obligations, it could be made clear that it is the husband who decides when a social visit ends in the case of her relatives, and the wife's word should be law when visiting his. (Or they could make it the other way around.)

Detailed family trees could be exchanged and studied, making it clear that Albert is an ex-alcoholic and must never be offered liquor, Jessie has the harelip and Tom the limp.

This way there could be fewer divorces.

Fewer marriages, too.

The young that love and leave

Sydney Morning Herald, 23 January 1986

Children grow up and leave the nest and parents mooch unhappily through the empty rooms for some time afterwards. Fairly often the children return for short and long spells and the parents mooch unhappily through the littered rooms, wondering why they wasted the time in mourning.

But mourn they do. And there is another lot they mourn for, other people's children who come for short and long spells, then go, mostly forever: the girl and boyfriends of sons and daughters.

Before you know it, they become part of the family. Their knickers and beach towels went in with the family wash. The husband and father, particularly if he has no daughters of his own, was enchanted with the young woman who served him his pudding first and took his side in arguments over television programs.

Then they are gone. They vanish just as the mother stops herself calling Philip Greg (the daughter's former boyfriend) and learns to say Tracey (the son's girlfriend) right off without running through Cathie, Lauren and Julie first. They are gone when she remembers at last that Philip eats baked pumpkin but can't stand parsnip and Tracey takes two sugars and no milk.

Quite often their presents stay as reminders. The terrible ashtrays and china animals offered bare from embarrassed hands because Tony (nicknamed Stonehead) wasn't strong on gift wrappings and things to write on cards. They had to be praised and put in conspicuous places, regardless of upsetting the existing decor. There they stay, long after Stonehead has mumbled his last goodbye because the mother has a warm spot for him and her heart broke a little with his.

Sometimes it is the natural children who are discarded; the ones that were absent for long spells, eating at someone else's table, buying unsuitable presents for someone else's mother, even mowing the lawn for someone else's father. Even though they're home all the time now, they are not seen that often — spending a lot of time behind a locked bedroom door, the listening family hearing the frequent squeaking of bed springs as the sufferer turns over and back, trying to leave the torment behind him.

Sometimes there are accidental meetings. Sometimes they are happy ones. The boy or girl who left or was left has a barrage of questions. Was the stairway ever put down from the dining room to the garage? Did the peach tree bear a good crop after they all had a hand in the pruning?

Other meetings are strained. There are no questions about the family because that would mean including Tom or Donna, Nick or Mary. No inquiries as to where they are going for the summer holidays because it was Terrigal last year and she went too.

She who might have been the mother-in-law worries when she is home that the other might cry a little when she too gets home.

For that's what *she* does.

The National Times

Australia's national weekly of business and affairs   ʸɔ *cents***

No. 777   DECEMBER 20 to 26, 1985

TRAVELLING TALES

In three "Style" columns dealing with travel in the **Sydney Morning Herald** in 1985 and 1986 Masters illustrates the way in which "home" is (paradoxically) the constant referent for most people when travelling. Home—the familiar and known place—is the heaven which we all carry about with us, a presence felt all the more substantially through its absence. "A flight of fantasy for the travel minded"—describing an extended in-flight fantasy—was probably based upon Masters' flight from Australia to London towards the end of 1985. The fantasy is a comic one of power over her children, a fantasy which gratifyingly includes the opportunity of bawling out everyone running the plane, from the pilot to the flight attendants.

From London Masters travelled to Russia for a two-week tour sponsored by the Literature Board of the Australia Council and the Soviet Writers" Union. Her companions were Tom Shapcott, director of the Literature Board, and Chris Wallace-Crabbe, Melbourne poet and academic. All three Australian writers were prompted to record their impressions. Masters' feature article, "Searching for the face of Soviet Literature", was published in the **National Times**; Shapcott wrote a "Russian Diary", and Wallace-Crabbe's response, an article entitled "Lost in Wonderland", was published in **Scripsi** magazine. Unlike her companions, Masters found the trip something of a purgatory, and her un-favourable impressions of the tour caused quite a controversy at the time, resulting in a follow-up letter from Shapcott to the **National Times** distancing the Literature Board from her account. For the most part, Russia seemed a loveless, illiberal country, its people poor and repressed—an impression also gained by a later Literature Board visitor, Blanche d'Alpuget, who found the people "withdrawn, patient, resigned" (**Good Weekend**, 24 September 1988). Both women felt themselves to be up against a secretive, closed face, but, while d'Alpuget imaged this confrontation as a strange communion with "the closed mythic darkness, the chthonic force" of Mother Russia, Masters felt affronted by the alienating and closed grey face of male officialdom. The only lines of dialogue open to her were with the women she met, and she felt frustrated by the general absence of young writers and artists. Of course, the solemn formalities engendered by an official tour were inevitable; Chris Wallace-Crabbe, who very much enjoyed the trip, nevertheless referred to "the scent of hierarchy in the air" and the conservatism of Moscow writing. Unlike Masters, though, Wallace-Crabbe was alert to the dangers of falling into clichés, such as the image of the Writers' Union as a group of elder powerbrokers, or the "naive division of people into bureaucrats and dissidents". In his later account of their brief tour, the difficulty of assessing the kind of intellectual climate in which Soviet writers lived and worked remained uppermost in his mind.

On the more positive side, away from official meetings with arts bureaucrats, Masters engaged in some lively exchanges about current Australian and Soviet writing. Responding to eager questioning from Anna Martinova, a journalist with the important paper **Literary Gazette**, she shone in talking about women's writing in Australia; and a week later, at the offices of the monthly English language journal **Soviet Literature**, she impressed everyone with her detailed knowledge of some recently published Soviet documentaries and short fiction. So gratified were her hosts that they asked her to write a piece for them which, according to Masters, would outline "the ways of the common people, the sharing of words and their meaning". The theme she chose to develop was the universal one of the need for care of the aged. Although she looked forward to meeting this request, there is no evidence to suggest that she managed to write the piece before her death ten months later.

In many ways the **National Times** article is close to the official report she was required to submit to the Literature Board. A number of departures should, however, be mentioned because they highlight various journalistic techniques. The visit to the Dostoyevsky museum, with its rather sentimental vignette of the writer's daughter pushing love notes under his study door, is new, as is her account of the Revolution Day parade on Red Square (a "heavy hardware ordeal" which fatigued her immensely, according to Wallace-Crabbe). The decor of Bella Ackmodolina's flat, noted in passing in the report, takes on a slightly nightmarish, even surreal, significance in the published article, and she also chose to highlight the longings she believed she saw in the faces of Russian women—their desire for world peace, or even for a different life outside the USSR.

If Masters' article reveals her lack of experience both as a world traveller and as a writer of politically sensitive journalism, she was nevertheless determined that other Literature Board travellers should profit by her expertise in domestic matters. The last paragraph of her official report reads:

On the **domestic front** in regard to travel in Russia, one should take soap, a small bath plug, toilet tissues, perhaps some teabags and coffee grounds, and Long Life milk is essential for tea and coffee is intolerable without it. Lifts can be slow in large hotels, so be fit enough to take the stairs. All hosts collecting us with cars were on time. I think it would be taken as a discourtesy to be late . . . Hotels were heated and only warm outdoor clothing like overcoat and hat were necessary. There did not appear to be dry cleaning services but there were laundry facilities advertised. We managed washing in our rooms and drying our things on towel rails. Food was quite good apart from the absence of fresh milk. There was no breakfast before 8 a.m., and snack bars as we know them are not plentiful... Not a place to go for pampering but an unforgettable experience for those lucky enough to be part of this exchange program.

Infrequent travellers — kleptomaniac and nervous

Sydney Morning Herald, 30 May 1985

You can tell the frequent travellers by the insides of their houses. There are no guest soaps stacked in the bathroom alongside shower-caps still in their transparent packs. No little plastic containers of honey and jam and Vegemite in the kitchen cupboards with mini-packs of cereals, nowhere about the house writing paper and envelopes engraved with the name of a hotel or motel.

All these goods can be found in the home of the infrequent travellers, those who spread their trips over two years or more, say to a funeral in Melbourne and a wedding in Queensland.

They no sooner fling their suitcase on the motel or hotel bed (discovering the rack provided for it only when they are about to leave) than they begin a prowl, scooping up what is there with the compliments of the management.

A cry of joy is not usually for the view from the window but for a find of chocolates or shampoo, rare bonuses for the infrequent travellers, who for economic reasons do not always get into the best places.

The side pocket of the luggage is soon bulging with packs of tea, coffee, sugar and everlasting milk ("we might have missed the milkman when we get back, Les").

Another practice of the infrequent travellers is arriving at the airport to catch a plane up to half a day before departure time.

They are often in the company of only the cleaners (who else would be there at 4 a.m. for an 8 a.m. flight?) and earn themselves hard, sharp looks from the first officials to arrive suspicious that there might be something of an explosive nature in their luggage.

Infrequent travellers hate being parted from their luggage, certain they will never see it again.

They rush to the conveyor belt and marvel at the nonchalant air of those (frequent travellers) whose gear can sail around and around while they drink coffee and make telephone calls.

For some unexplained reason, the luggage of infrequent travellers comes out last. Then when they dive for it and sweep it away they are not certain it is theirs. A check of the side pocket reveals the deodorant stick they flung in when on the last trip to the bathroom before leaving home, a half-empty pack of aspirin and a wad of paper tissues.

But wouldn't everyone, just about everyone, have scruffed grey nylon bags, and everyone, just about everyone, be unable to remember whether the deodorant stick, aspirin and tissues went in when the packing started three weeks ago?

The relief is enormous when the hotel is reached and the bag torn open and up pops the flannelette pyjamas and twenty-year-old dressing gown.

The trauma over the tickets continues throughout the stay. They are certain, absolutely certain, the clerk tore out the return ticket as well as the other before they boarded the plane. They didn't dare check when they were in their seat, because they would have to curb an urge to run to the pilot and demand he turn around and go back.

They spend the entire visit avoiding the compartment or handbag or wallet where it should be (if it wasn't dropped and lost in the rush on to the plane in fear of being left behind).

Infrequent travellers seldom bring themselves to use the jam, Vegemite, shampoo, etc, souvenired.

We like to keep them as mementos of our rare and wonderful trips.

That dream of a lifetime that isn't

Sydney Morning Herald, 27 March 1986

A man went around the world on his life's savings and wherever he was, in Paris, Rome, or looking up at the Himalayas, he always said the same thing: "It's all right, I suppose. But it isn't like Ballarat."

He came from Ballarat. But he might have been from Condobolin, Revesby or The Esperance. It wasn't like home. And that's where he'd rather be.

People spend millions on travel and millions of them suffer it like the purgatory they must endure to gain entry to heaven. It goes without saying, heaven is home.

They make their earthly record even worse by lying in

their teeth, which are probably false too by the time they realise that what they have been calling for years their Dream of a Lifetime isn't.

"Worth every cent," they say when they get home and find the house intact, not burgled or burnt to the ground as they feared every waking hour of their time away.

The fears invade their sleeping hours too, in spite of a better quality mattress than the old one at home.

The rain in Ireland sets them wondering if any has got into the lounge room through a casement window that doesn't close properly. Or whether the precious pot plants have died of neglect in spite of the watering can and plant food bought at great cost.

The travel people lie in their teeth too, theirs being pearly white filled with the best-quality enamel and shown a lot. Or more fairly they tell all those half-truths.

Sample the exotic foods of Asia. (When you get home Mum's fried flathead in batter will never taste better.)

Experience the pampering at the best hotels in the world. (Think of the joy of being back home, littering the floor with your clothes, no longer in fear of what the maids will think and shame at the grey shade of your underwear drying on the room heater.)

There would not be any great loss of business if they did come right out and say things like this.

Come on a Discovery Tour with us. (Then discover for yourself how good home is.)

They could add another couple of lines.

We guarantee you your old place on the bowling club committee on your return.

That would guarantee them a sell-out.

A flight of fantasy for the travel minded

Sydney Morning Herald, 6 March 1986

One of the few good things about long aeroplane travel is the time and scope for fantasy. I like to imagine the aircraft is my home skyward bound, and the crew my family. There are enough to fill this need: Roy, Ian, Quentin, Chris, Sue, Deb and Michael. This flight of fantasy sets off with the plane.

"Cabin crew attend to doors!" Here we go. Agitated, I count the heads of crew in sight to make sure they are not all bossily clicking overhead lockers shut, stuffing your best coat to the back as if it were an old dusting rag. It would be terrible if everyone left everyone else to do the doors. You might set out for the toilet and end up on some remote island in the Indian Ocean.

Roy would take on that role of announcing the progress of the journey. Ping, ping, ping would go the bell and he would preserve a respectable silence, believing our breaths were held for what was coming next in his aren't-I-the-best-captain-in-the-world voice.

"Put a sock in it!" I would be able to yell back when he gave out that useless information about the weather in London, told us it was cloud below (in case we thought it a flock of sheep) followed by all those syrupy apologies about being five minutes behind schedule, and the air turbulence we had to endure when he should know the bumping about saved us from lapsing into unconsciousness through boredom.

The others would have charge of the food trolley. No longer would I need to lower my tray at the first creak of wheels and bore the half-darkness with my eyes in terror at being overlooked. I would not need to thank them like a grateful whimpering pup for the thimbleful of coffee they called a refill.

"Revolting!" I would say when I passed them the ruin of my meal. Not that that spirited lot would remain silent.

"Serves you right! You're not supposed to eat the cardboard!"

"Bring a hacksaw next time for the bread rolls!" I would call to their fast-vanishing posteriors.

The fantasy would terminate near the journey's end, the dream of having them all under my thumb for the first and only time in forty years.

"Cabin crew! Doors to manual!" only serves to remind me of the difficulties associated with getting offspring to manually operate doors. My husband Charles, father of the brood, has called out thousands of times in all those years of rearing: "Feel that wind like a stepmother's breath! Who was in last and didn't shut the door?"

In the aircraft, not a budge from anyone. Eyes would remain glued to the television. Just as we got to the good part of the movie we would all slide out and finish up somewhere on a remote island in the Indian Ocean.

Searching for the face of Soviet literature

National Times, 20-26 December 1985

In Russia we were shown somewhat briefly, for time did not permit long and searching looks, the face of Soviet literature, circa 1985. Or, perhaps we should say, the one face of Soviet literature with many expressions.

The stolid, the cautious, the inquiring, the alert, the eager, the glimpse of friendliness, the tragic.

The face, whatever other expression it wore, never

failed to reflect courtesy of the highest kind, whether it was the Soviet Writers' Union the hosts, magazines or newspapers, their table spread most generously with grapes, apples and matchless Russian chocolates with close attention to our teacups.

The message was clear. Our visit was of great importance.

At these arranged meetings of Soviet Writers' Unions (in Moscow, Leningrad and Tashkent) we saw, or rather I felt I saw, the closed and stolid face.

They were without exception elderly men. Grey men. No women. On the wall of the Writers' Union Club in Moscow more than one hundred photos of male writers. Few young or even youngish faces. Only one woman's portrait in a corner. No look of triumph having made it to this male dominated sanctuary, but a sort of pained nervousness there, like a guest at a party by mistake.

Rightly or wrongly one is made to feel that this panel of men run a tightly controlled (literary) ship, kept sternly on course.

In an exchange of information on writing and publishing in our respective countries we asked about opportunities for and encouragement of young writers in Soviet Russia. We were assured such programs were operating.

But nowhere was our attention drawn to any named young and exciting new writer perhaps with an award (we were told they were given quite liberally) for poetry or prose.

Have you a Kate Grenville or a Tim Winton? I longed to ask.

Nowhere did we hear, for all the Russians' devotion to the theatre — opera, dance and drama — of any new experimental writer whose work was performed and acclaimed.

There may be a healthy growth of youthful writing being nurtured. We may have missed the nursery in our tour. Perhaps it was like an old-fashioned visit to relatives where the adults entertained and the children were kept out of sight.

In Leningrad in the Writers' Union building we were shown a quite curious Soviet expression. I mentioned with sympathy the obvious gaps through the Nazi siege of 1941-45. We saw the memorial to thousands who died, the little building with a scant collection of photographs depicting the deprivations of those terrible times. A glass case enclosing a stub of candle and a crust of bread. The beautifully kept grounds were a common grave. Countless dead.

But the spokesman said no, no writers were lost. They worked as journalists, correspondents and in allied (and protected) occupations. What? No talent decayed there under that sheet of snow? None with their tales yet to tell? Is Soviet thinking generally as closed at that? Would post-Revolution writing be akin to it?

Another curious expression, stubborn, part-scornful on the face of Moscow radio interviewer George Murzin, who described Mayakovsky's poetry as "early revolutionary stuff".

"He died before the revolution really matured," he said.

We discovered for ourselves Mayakovsky's statue of giant proportions outside our hotel. Our attention was not drawn to it.

Nor were we shown the Chekhov museum, although the ever-alert Chris Wallace-Crabbe tracked it down.

But we were shown the Dostoyevsky museum, the first-floor flat where he lived with his family. Full credit must go to those responsible for the careful restoration of the trappings of the life of the author most famous for his *Crime and Punishment*.

Love was not overlooked in the scheme. Among the

pens, the curled pages and the hand-made cigarettes were notes from Dostoyevsky's little daughter. He could not spare much time for his family and kept his study door tightly shut. The notes were pushed under his door. "We love you, Daddy," they read.

There was something to lighten the face of Soviet Russia. You do not see much evidence of love. People seem to walk the streets singly, rather stolidly. Husbands do not push prams. Young couples do not wrap their arms around each other.

So the word love lightened the gloom of Dostoyevsky's museum (and here it might be noted that it only recently became an official part of tourists' agendas). There was the universal cry of "Give me some of your time, Daddy! Tell me you love me!"

The redoubtable George offered another morsel for us to digest. He offered a book for reviewing, with a promise to broadcast the review after translation into Russian. The book was by an expatriate Californian, living and working as a journalist in Moscow. The subject was child rearing in Soviet Abkhasia, an autonomous republic in the Caucasus.

"If you find it dull," he said, "I will send you another to review."

We were reminded of our right back home to say a book was dull if we found it so. May we always cherish such freedom.

I believe I found the healthiest side of Soviet literature on the faces of the women we met. Of course none were established women writers taking part in the formal meetings. They were translators, interpreters, secretaries, organisers of the project in which we were involved. They hummed in the background, seeing to our needs. One or two ventured to murmur they wrote a little poetry and short fiction. They sounded as if they were clumsily trying to imitate a Pavlova.

I thought many of these women splendid. Anna Martinova was one. She was a journalist heading the international section of the *Literary Gazette* in Moscow. Behind her flood of questions on the status of women's writing in Australia I detected an urgent appeal to Russian women to make their mark on Soviet literature. She gave over a page of her newspaper to extracts from our books. She came to the hotel with photographs for us taken by the newspaper. She seemed as if she wanted to talk forever.

Again we saw women in action for the cause of better understanding between our two countries through published and translated works at the office of *Soviet Literature*, the monthly magazine available in Australia. There seemed a dominance of females producing this magazine of poetry and prose.

Notable among published works in recent issues was "War's Unwomanly Face", a collection of interviews with Soviet women who fought at the front during the Nazi siege, or as they say in Russia, The Great Patriotic War.

A young woman journalist, Svetlana Alexiyevich, presents these reminiscences with energy and compassion, avoiding the morbid, harrowing as the experiences were. The collection is also available as a book and should be compulsory reading for everyone.

Around the table were the daughters of this generation's women, their spirit reflected on those gentle womanly faces, words the weapons they were seeking to use in their quest for peace.

The tragic face of Soviet literature was that of poet Bella Ackmodolina. We are indebted to Chris Wallace-Crabbe for this meeting, her address given through a mu-

tual colleague in Australia. She lives with her husband
Boris, a theatre designer, on the top floor of a derelict
Moscow building.

We met the pair with Bella's fellow writers, whose
work is turned down for publication by the Writers'
Union. Their collected works appear in a handsomely
bound book, *Metropole,* and is banned by the Writers'
Union.

What excuse is offered for this treatment of Bella
Ackmodolina, once recognised as one of Russia's finest
poets? The answer would be, we were told: She was a
good writer once. Now she is a drunk.

Literary history is peppered with such people, their
works legendary.

The pity of the scene was the conflict of loyalties. All
of these people loved Russia with a similar passion for
one's own country as that expressed by our writers —
Lawson, Katharine Susannah Prichard, down to the
moderns.

Their cultural starvation contrasted with the food they
spread for us. Russians have a reputation for spending a
week's salary on the best caviar, smoked salmon and
grapefruit for their guests and eating frugally for the next
six days.

The decor of the room spelled out their message. On
one wall was a huge stone crucifix, Jesus with bowed and
sorrowing head. On the other, so close by there was room
for only two people between the two, a bear skin of similar size. The teeth were bared and sharp, as were the un-
relenting eyes.

As the night wore on, Bella's unaccepted verse read
aloud, the gloom deepened and it was hard to believe the
face of Jesus did not droop lower and the lips of the bear
lift in a more cruel snarl.

The tour program, to the credit of the organisers, included visits to galleries, museums, and exhibitions, apart from those of a literary nature.

We saw behind the restoration of such palaces as that of Catherine the Great in Leningrad the sacrifices of the people to allow the billions of roubles to be spent this way.

On the other hand, at Tashkent, there was the well-designed Museum of Economics, and here we saw proof of the industry and dedication on the people's part to contribute to world markets as well as self-support.

The spirit of the people seemed indomitable. You saw them as strong and honest. What a triumph it would be to be able to say the same of post-Revolution writing.

But we need an increased flow of translated works to see for ourselves what is being said or written. We need to increase the current somewhat tentative flow of Australian works for them to see what we are up to.

They readily dropped the names of Prichard, Alan Marshall, Dymphna Cusack, Judah Waten, most of whom had visited there. It is fairly easy to become familiar with writers met. We need to show them the works of our moderns, including those of our budding young.

They might then be encouraged to expose more of theirs.

Everywhere we went our Aborigines were mentioned. I think we all shared some embarrassment that interest expressed in their culture was greater than that of many of our near neighbours at home.

This piece would be incomplete without reference to Natasha, our interpreter. She looked like a ballerina with her white skin, black hair parted in the centre, slim and shapely figure, giving lie to the theory that Russian girls are frumpish and unattractive.

She lived with her widowed mother in a two-roomed flat and no matter how late the hour when our official engagements were completed she took the last train home with amazing good cheer. ''If I miss it, I'll sit in the waiting room until morning,'' she said.

She had no phone and shared her bedroom with her mother. She spoke fluent English and has just about mastered Italian. Between stints as an interpreter she works in an office at a job she hates. Her dream is to one day set foot in France, Italy or America. She said, with her wide and aching smile, her chances were slim indeed.

Perhaps I could also add that we were in Moscow for Revolution Day on November 7 and had tickets to Red Square to see the parade. Thousands watched, thousands took part. The city closed its doors for the celebrations. We tried at the Australian Embassy to make telephone calls to London and Australia but were told, although it was early the previous evening, we would need to wait until life returned to normal the day after.

The militia marched with such precision their overcoats rippled as evenly as if a breeze ran through them. Guns boomed, smoke swirled and missiles and other warfare grew larger and more menacing as the parade reached its climax. Then the people surged on to the ground carrying paper carnations big as young trees.

Where did they store them in their tiny flats massed in a huge housing development on the outskirts of the town?

''By 1990 everyone will be housed,'' we were told.

It sounded as if the people were akin to those wooden Russian dolls that unscrew to fit more dolls inside.

Will Natasha's daughter, if she has one, carry a carnation, too, on Revolution Day? Will she stand in the cold as thousands of children did that day mouthing the words that came over the public address system, faces nearly as still and stern as those of the marching soldiers?

Will she be content with a shared room, no car to drive,

a goodbye to an American boyfriend she will never see again?

Perhaps it's there, in those multi-storey flats, that the real Russian army is in training for a new revolution.

Home Style
Renovators of an
old house go for
Baroque —
Page 3

The Sydney Morning Herald

Style

THURSDAY, JUNE 20, 1985

THINGS · PEOPLE · DO

OPINION

Rituals, habits, conventions of attitude, speech and dress: how badly they sometimes serve us, and yet how essential many of them are for rubbing along from day to day. Masters' sharp ear for the vernacular peculiar to certain times and places (she would never have used the phrase "You've got to be joking" in her fictional dialogue of the 1930s) made her shrink in the 1980s from the false Americanism "Have a nice day". Just as false could be the perennial response "Very well, thank you" to enquiries about health, but this well-worn lie was one she endorsed as an essential strategy for survival.

While the habit of covering up might steal upon us with the years, there was no covering up an abrupt and ungracious descent into old age. Fashion, an ill-fitting garment at the best of times, might erupt in a pure flukery of colour-coordinated stockings and accessories, but towards the end of our long time dying there can be no disguising the inevitable: "sans teeth, sans eyes, sans taste, sans everything".

It's difficult going cold turkey with your butcher

Sydney Morning Herald, 20 June 1985

First the father influences the lives of women, next the husband or lover and after that the gynaecologist.

You could add the butcher to the list. He wears a white coat as does the gynaecologist and they both wear similar expressions of concern and confidence. She is the only woman in the world who matters, whether the hands are gently seeking the position of the foetus or stroking the topside of veal she is planning for dinner.

Women rarely leave their gynaecologists unless they die or go to live abroad.

Many would like to add to their family, but simply can't face it without Dr X.

They cast reproachful glances at husbands who dare upset this plan by taking promotion and moving too far away to make the relationship practical.

Women can make a clean break with their butcher when this happens and sometimes they are greatly relieved, for after ten, twenty or more years they are due for a change.

Business either falls off and he starts passing off inferior cuts, or it grows and he can't give her the personal service he once did.

But she finds it hard to sneak out of his life forever, and take on Graham down the road who has opened Superior Meats, because her old butcher hardly ever fails to bob out of the cold room when she is there about to give the thumbs down to the mince steak which looks as if he has taken to it with a bottle of cochineal and a paint brush.

He rushes up with a cry of welcome and orders the staff to take great care of his oldest and most valued customer.

She melts and takes two kilograms of the mince, remembering all they had been through together, like the knuckles of veal he saved for her to make broth when her babies were small (although they spat it out) and the way he cut her steak and kidney up so finely and told her when she was a bride how long to cook the corned beef.

Eventually though, her order dwindles to half a kilogram of sausages a week, gabbling an excuse that she and the dog are the only ones at home, then when she makes the final break she often has to give away the whole block of shops.

If she goes to the dry cleaner next door she is in danger of being seen, her old butcher showing a mournful face in the window, pale like the fat on his half side of rump, accusing her of desertion.

She ponders whether to go and front him, and say the family has turned vegetarian, but the fad is sure to pass and she will be back.

She would probably come away with a side of lamb, two calves' livers, two kilograms of gravy beef and the frozen turkey he failed to sell at Easter.

You would expect a sense of great relief should a sign go up "Under new management".

But her sense of guilt is enormous. She might have driven him to bankruptcy and she pictures him cleaning bloodied floors at some menial task in some abattoir. Still missing her.

Television presents a cold front

Sydney Morning Herald, 19 April 1985

All those millions of dollars spent on television sounds like a terrible waste. The sets in the living rooms, now invading bedrooms as well, the satellite hook up to every corner of the world.

Those good-looking men and women telling us about it from the screen and having noughts added to their salaries as their popularity grows (and to keep up with salaries paid by rival channels).

Us? Who's that? Nobody watches television.

"Don't turn that thing on whatever you do!" wife orders husband jabbing the air with a handful of forks. Two couples are coming to dinner and she is setting the table in a dark mood for the Beef Wellington is not turning out well.

The set, wearing a dark face too, appears to shrink into the corner in shame.

The wife considers throwing an Indian rug over it to impress the guests with this show of contempt.

Husband has been sneakily watching a show, though. He swaps some comments on it with one of the typists at work, throwing furtive glances over his shoulder in case there are people around who go to Joan Sutherland concerts, have season tickets to the rugby union and read Beatrix Potter and R.L. Stevenson in family groups after dinner.

"I don't actually watch it," the man says when typewriters fade out and other heads bend closer. "I switch on a bit early in case I miss the news."

People sit in trains and buses and on ferries scanning the metres of print in newspapers and magazines devoted to television programs and people appearing in them.

They keep an eye out for anyone looking over their shoulders, and turn with great haste to the editorial pages if they detect anything like an expression of conspiracy.

If that fellow thinks he's going to strike up a conversation with me about *A Country Practice* or *Family Ties* or rubbish like that he's in for a shock, says the rattle of paper and the face now pressed close to columns on the new Russian leader or current art shows in New York, Washington and Edinburgh.

What about the weather?

There must be a million spent on salaries and equipment to bring to the screen those details on cloud formation, cold fronts and troughs and currents going every whichway.

But who takes it all in?

People meeting in the street raise the subject of the weather as they have been doing since long before newsprint, let alone television.

"We're in for a spot of rain, I reckon."

"Reckon so. The old knees are playing up no end."

"What's the forecast anyway?"

"Wouldn't have a clue."

It makes you sad to think of people like that lovely silver-haired gentleman with those beautifully drawn maps earnestly explaining happenings from the Gulf of Carpentaria to the Tasman Sea. (He looks the kind who would give up an afternoon's fishing to visit an aging aunt in the western suburbs and remain gracious and smiling throughout the ordeal.)

"Good evening everyone," he always starts off.

Everyone?

That's no one, if you ask everyone.

Where have all the old crocks gone?

Sydney Morning Herald, 22 August 1985

We must be the healthiest nation in the world if you go by conversations overheard in supermarkets and other places where people gather, with and without shopping carts.

"How is all the family?" one asks another after the cries of fancy-meeting-you-heres have been submerged by several excuse-mes and do-you-minds in the martyred tones of those anxious to get the job done and out of the place.

The two settle themselves as flat as they can against the breakfast cereals and join their carts end-to-end, making it impossible for others to stock up on rolled oats and Wheaty Bites.

"Oh, everyone is well. Very well!" is the cry, followed by the query "And all of yours?"

"Well, too. Everyone is well!" comes the triumphant reply.

This can be a dampener if you are trying to squeeze past to get to the pain-killing tablets, disinfectants, bandages, cotton wool for stuffing ears, and chest rubs and eucalyptus for an outbreak of influenza.

You pause to look upon these people blessed with such an ailment-free existence. They are usually rotund, very cheerful looking. It would be a relief to see creases in their clothes where they might have spent several hours waiting outside surgeries. It would be comforting to be able to conclude positively they were lying in their smiling teeth.

Come to think of it, this sort of thing goes on in doctors' waiting rooms too. After the opener of fancy-meeting-you-here, there is the inevitable follow up: "And how is all the family?'' and the reply: "Well. Everyone is very well!''

No effort is made to hide the X-ray package as large as a billiard table, and sealed envelopes addressed to Dr Bloggs, that one or the other (often both) is toting.

You get the same change from the children. They gambol about playing hide-and-seek behind chairs, to the despair of mothers trying to keep them neat and languid to justify the appointment.

"And how are you today?" you tentatively offer.

"Good! Real good!" comes hurtling back at you, swifter than a kookaburra diving on a grub. To drive the point home, the speaker turns into an aeroplane wheeling arms for wings and upsets a table full of magazines.

The same in chemists' shops. There, with hands dripping doctors prescriptions, you crash into someone similarly armed and the cries are exchanged. "Yes, we're all well. Tip top. Bursting with health!"

Each head swings away then in the direction of sun hats, footwear, washing-up detergent and all the other odd things chemists sell these days, letting it be known that is what they are there for.

But think of the alternative. How is all the family?

Terrible! Most of us up all night with dysentery. Can I be served before you? I'm hurrying to see Uncle Albert before he's wheeled in for surgery. Even the cat is waiting to go to the vet at our place.

Deceitful, lying, cheating lot that we are, let's keep it that way.

If you say have a nice day, I won't

Sydney Morning Herald, 19 September 1985

This rampaging practice of wishing people a nice day must be in line for reviewing. It most likely started in America, which also gave us takeaway hamburgers, and soon, it is understood, throw-away contact lenses.

We hardly ever fail to follow the trail.

Have-a-nice-day was first encountered when we visited the United States some years ago. In a Los Angeles supermarket we were attended to by a woman made up to look like Ali McGraw, who was then fashionable on the big screen. Seeing her take a pencil from her stiff black hair you suspected she had been through the Jane Wyman era and may have gone back as far as Mary Pickford.

She added the tax to our bill as you would put a pinch of poison to a nicely served-up plate of curry-and-rice.

It was our first meeting with this kind of thing. It was a terrible let down. We had yelped with pure joy at the price of the cheese and chocolate-chip cookies, and here they were, with the tax turning out dearer than Franklins back home.

The woman did not wish us a nice day, but the store supervisor, seeing the omission, rushed up and obliged.

"God-damn-it I keep forgetting," the woman muttered. The benevolent look the man gave us turned nasty as soon as he got his eyes back on her.

Later, here in Australia, in supermarkets and other places, have-a-nice-day was in full cry.

"Have-a-nice-day-can-I-see-inside-your-bag-please?" the checkout girl would say in tones similar to those used in discussion with her checkout neighbour on the state of her feet, the mother-in-law coming to the end of a long baby-sitting stint, or the live-in boyfriend failing to come up with his share of the rent.

Quite often you are going along fairly well until this gibberish starts.

The child has not woken with an illness akin to dengue fever, the third pair of hose the toe was jabbed into showed no runs when dragged on full stretch, and the dandruff appears under control.

Then someone throws a have-a-nice-day in your face and the doubts set in. Maybe this was the only part of it you would survive. When things start off well they have a habit of turning sour. God knows what's ahead. You begin to pale and perspire at what might develop as the day does.

Have-a-nice-day comes out like an order sometimes, rather than a wish. Those sergeant-major types commanding office vestibules and bus terminals bark it out in such a way you scuttle off, beginning to worry that you are not trying hard enough. You get guilt pangs about looking forward to a bus ride wallowing in misery, looking around for the grimmest headlines the papers have to offer, watching out for comforting messages like The End Of The World Is At Hand scrawled overnight on a factory wall.

The babble about having a nice day doesn't let up all morning. It's played out around the tea urn, at the petrol pumps, and the chemist joins the chorus having just filled your prescription for weeping armpits, head noises or fallen arches.

There is a lull around midday before it turns to have-a-nice-afternoon, and just when you are pretty sure you forgot to take the chops out of the freezer and to let the cat out, someone is certain to start urging you to have-a-nice-evening.

You realise then that you have failed to hold your end

up. Not once throughout the day, in your preoccupied self-centred fashion, did you wish anyone a nice one.

God-damn-it.

All dressed up with nowhere to stow

Sydney Morning Herald, 9 May 1985

When I am dressing to go out somewhere I very often think of the Queen. Her Majesty, the Queen, since I am aware there are other kinds. It must be a devil of a job for her getting everything right.

She goes to first nights, the opening of parliament, inspects the ravages of flood and famine, flies to Canada fairly often and to Australia occasionally. I go to shop for birthday presents, visit a sick aunt, one or another of my children, a new baby when they have one.

If the Queen leaves home for days or weeks, she has half a plane-load of clothes and an army of dressers. A similar service operates at home. But always, I imagine, whether for a garden party or a hop to Africa, the final choice of outfit is up to her.

"If Smithers lays out that mulberry thing I'll wrap it around her neck," she might say to His Highness in the privacy of their room. He might reply with cautious questioning on her choice. When she answers, there is that silence familiar in all homes where families have a combined revulsion for an orange stripe or brown floral and can't wait for its relegation to the rag collection.

But the Queen is in an enviable position when it comes to handbags. She appears only to have to get the colour right and not worry about the size.

I do not know if she stuffs an old pair of Philip's underpants inside to get that nicely puffed-out look, but it would not be due to your average handbag's contents.

Bags can be a headache for ordinary people. Mentally selecting an outfit on waking on the day of the engagement, or while tearing through the house tidying it up before departing, I have fooled myself into thinking I have it right.

My grey suit with the red shoes and grey stockings and the red bag on a long shoulder strap. I am ready to reach for the bag when I become aware of its size and shape, round like a bread-and-butter plate and about as thick through.

And out on the kitchen table I have an apple pie to take to Roy who favours a slice when he has to skip dinner and leave early for football training, and a bundle of cuttings for the keen gardener in the family, the soil already weeping black tears through the sodden paper bag.

I have to start all over again and match some clothes to a bag that will accommodate such loot.

Once I had an enormous triumph. If I had a Smithers I would have called to her to exclaim with me over my green pantihose — so perfectly matched to my green skirt that came up well, in spite of its age, after a good dry clean.

And I was able to drop into my black bag with the green stripe the coconut ice I'd made for the twin grandchildren and two picture books.

Smithers would have agreed that congratulations to the supplier of the hose were in order with an assurance of continued royal patronage.

In this case though, it was a pair from the chain-store — originally coloured pebble or sand — which became entangled in the washing machine with a green chenille quilt.

You *know* you're getting old when . . . your clothes come back in fashion and your feet change colour

Sydney Morning Herald, 21 March 1985

When are we old? At what time does youth cut off and old age begin? And don't argue that there is a gradual process through middle age. Such a state no longer exists.

Have you seen those pictures in the newspapers of family groups, in which the mother of the twenty-year-old looks even younger than her daughter? You have to go for your glasses and check a caption to avoid confusing a twelve-year-old with her grandmother.

Some women of sixty are wearing spikey, two-toned hair, and men the same age have chains around their necks and shirts open to the navel.

But it has to happen. One day you are old and the next you are older.

Do you know why a lot of old people get up early in the morning? Their first thought on waking is they are a day older and they need to move fast in case they are cheated of tomorrow.

They start going to more funerals. They listen to the eulogy about the deceased and relate it to themselves, substituting their names for that of old Maud or Albert.

Would they measure up so well? They doubt it and hurry away, both to get working on creating a better record of commendable deeds and to avoid close contact with the coffin, the birthdate on the brass plaque a year later than their own.

Christmas and birthdays bring little joy. The gifts often appear destined to outlive the recipient, like large books with fine print which will take to the year 2000 to finish, and plants in pots that will still be blooming about the same time.

Sons and daughters suggest you extend the house upwards, sideways or out the back for flat accommodation for a helpful little income. Also helpful should a new money-spinning scheme fail to spin and there is the need for cheap housing at short notice.

But the idea fails to appeal. There would be all that hammering and banging and pouring of concrete, all those trips to the local council, all those telephone calls to plumbers and electricians, and the day after the massive clean-up is complete, the aging parent could you-know-what.

They know they are growing old when they start swimming later and later each summer. And there is this perplexing thought that they have forgotten something as they are about to go in the water.

Glasses? No, they are back on the sand in a fold of the garment since visibility has been reduced to the son or daughter there hanging on to an arm in fear of the first breaker whisking them off to New Zealand.

Footwear still on? No, the feet show up magenta-coloured except around the corns which are standing out egg-yolk yellow, like those silent cops that used to be at busy street intersections.

So what is it? It's the dentures they had fitted since they swam last year. They dive in and swim with jaws clamped tight, in case they lose them.

If they make it back to the beach next summer there could be a hearing aid to deal with as well.

Life jogs past your window in early morning

Sydney Morning Herald, 31 January 1985

In twenty-four hours there is morning, afternoon and night, so people say.

Wrong, wrong.

There is early morning and Rest of the Day.

Early morning is when the joggers are out and a woman takes a cup of tea to the front veranda and waves to them without a cigarette in her hand.

Her youngest child hears the early morning noises and gets up. He hears the slap, slap, slap of the joggers' feet and the huh, huh, huh of their breathing.

He hears the birds buried in the bottlebrush, making their early morning noises, like scissors cutting fine silk.

He takes his box of building toys and sits near his mother on the cold tiles, and sniffs a lot, rubbing his hand across his nose. She does not tell him to get a dressing gown and a handkerchief.

She sees dew on her camellia tree hung as neatly on the leaves as the glass beads that trimmed the covers for the jugs of milk in her grandmother's kitchen.

"See the dew buds?" she says to the child and he looks and asks if they will stay there all day.

The joggers stop, one meeting the other on the footpath and each lifts his sweaty face in the direction of the telegraph wires overhead.

Two birds are hanging up there, hanging in the air, suspended like swimmers on a great pure wave of sky, dark little birds needing only to move their little red claws and lift their wings, light as a baby's breath to stay there.

The joggers each give a little shake of their heads, keeping their feet in motion, before shooting off.

Who was that man, each one thinks. A surgeon, a garbage collector, a company secretary? (It doesn't matter.)

The woman dreams through a second cup of tea. She will make good use of the day, weed the rose beds, write to her sister in Scotland, go through her wardrobe and give some of her clothes to Lifeline, make a proper pudding for dinner.

Soon there is too much noise to think on. Up the street the bus has stopped, a roar in its chest and a great shaking of its rear. People press around the door, and car brakes screech as a latecomer tears across the street to get there before the bus doors clamp shut.

"Come on!" says the woman to the little boy and grabs his arm. She takes up her cigarette pack on the way to the kitchen.

The little boy catches the school bus and sits with his too-large case on his knees, his big eyes under his too-large hat, frightened about the lessons he can't do.

The jogger in his collar and tie and with his briefcase joins the queue for the ferry.

The collar is too tight and he is sure the briefcase is missing a file needed for a ten o'clock meeting. He sees the file in his imagination on top of his bureau at home and has to stop his hands opening the case and clawing through the contents.

He wishes he was the garbage man (who has gone back to bed).

The water slapping the wharf is cold and dark, already with two drink cans and an empty cigarette pack bobbing on it.

Early morning is over. The Rest of the Day has begun.

Austinmer

Sydney Morning Herald, 1 January 1986

You could shelter under a man's black umbrella on Austinmer beach, wear pre-war woollen bathers and have no
better suntan than a seagull and you wouldn't feel out of
place.

Austinmer, on the south coast of New South Wales, is
everyone's beach — cosy and intimate as your own backyard and not much larger.

The old dressing sheds are still there like the wing of a
family home no one has the heart to pull down although
the children have all gone.

Inside are the long forms where ladies laid their silk and
voile dresses, their rolled-up stockings and stays and
turned their faces to the wall to pull on their bathers with
wide shoulders and skirts all around. Outside is the long
veranda where they met their men coming from their side
in their heavy woollen trunks and long trousers and cam-
bric shirts in a tight roll under their arms.

You could carry on that way today. No one would take
any notice.

Illywhacker

Fremantle Arts Review, vol. 1 no. 1, January 1986

We need a fat book now and again.

We need a balance against the spate of slender works,
perhaps more suited to our rushed lifestyle.

We are rapidly becoming a weary lot, even the burden
of holding a big book for a read in bed becomes a daunt-
ing prospect.

Publishers are reeling off the shorter novel, books close in size to the novella.

We can call to mind Malouf's *Fly Away Peter,* Garner's *The Children's Bach* and Anderson's *Tirra Lirra by the River.*

Nothing can be taken from the quality of these works (and others) concentrated as they are, flesh stripped from the bones, one paragraph often doing the work of several pages.

While Peter Carey's *Illywhacker* does not conform to the read-on-the-run fiction for the eighties, it is not obese, not over endowed with flesh for all its physical bulk running to six hundred pages.

Apparently few have baulked at the bulk. Only three months into print *Illywhacker* (University of Queensland Press) re-issued.

Should one explain (yet again) an *Illywhacker,* the term for a con man or trickster? The popularity of the novel should render this unnecessary. One wonders if a new slang will be launched (''Don't listen to that old illywhacker!'' or ''Spare us the illywhacking!'')

Carey says a lot in his opening line. My name is Herbert Badgery. I am one hundred and thirty nine years old and something of a celebrity.

A liar and a skite, dear reader. Make up your mind whether to read on.

Of course you do, like the wise parent of a child with bad habits. Better to look for the reasons than thump him across the ear.

Carey has you chuckling right off. He describes his hero's decrepit state . . . ''like some old squid decaying on a beach . . . a dick as scaley and scabby as a horse's''.

Even without an introduction to this writer through his earlier *Bliss* and *The Fat Man in History,* readers getting into the Fat Book of (literary) History would soon become absorbed by his insight into people and places.

He can be brief, calling a character (Ernest Vogelnest) a "funny looking little coot" or more expansive as with Phoebe, Badgery's first love.

> The chin and lips were perfect, as if the imaginary almighty had lavished extravagant amounts of time on them, and then realising it was getting late, had rushed onto the small nose and forehead, cramming them in where there was hardly room.

Carey introduces us to the O'Hagens when Badgery goes to their farm to sell them a Ford. A Tin Lizzie as it was known then. More illwhackery here, for his prime objective was to seduce Mrs O'Hagen. We are then given (here and elsewhere) a slice of Australian history, a look at the days when Australia was being developed by families in the scrub living in shacks they built themselves from timber cleared to plough the earth, when sons stayed down on the farm, with no choice but to work along with fathers from the time they were old enough to hold an axe.

"I could hear the ring of axes," Carey writes, opening his chapter, opening our ears to the loneliness and the isolation.

Unfortunately he did not find Mrs O'Hagen home. Or fortunately for us, for Badgery may have found greater joy with her in the bedroom and we would have been deprived perhaps of an encounter with the male O'Hagens. There was Stu the father, Goog and Gus the sons, backwoodsmen Australian style.

Badgery begins his sales pitch by agreeing to help with the clearing. The way of course, to sell anything in those times from motor cars to packets of pins was to offer a willing pair of hands to mend a chair, nurse a baby, wipe dishes, in a household desperate for extra hands in a working week that knew no let up.

Stu prepared the maggot-ridden leg of lamb for the oven (any visitors including salesmen were asked to share the meal) by bashing it against the veranda post. Yes, fly-blown meat was often part of the diet of our pioneering forebears.

So there are facts of life in plenty in *Illywhacker* along with the lies of the hero. Nor were they his province only.

Lover Leah Goldstein told them in letters to Badgery during his term in jail. She described the weather as good when it was bad, herself as well when she wasn't. She wrote about long walks on the cliff tops in Bondi with Rosa, giving the impression they had just taken place, while Rosa was gravely sick in hospital.

Here Carey alerts us to the liar in us all. For who amongst us hasn't written in similar vein, delivering only happiness to comfort and cheer?

The book is dedicated to Carey's parents, a couple one would imagine who lived through the Depression, the reign of Jack Lang, events leading up to the Second World War, Sydney's lifestyle in the thirties, quite some time before the birth of their son.

Perhaps part of the dedication and thanks are in appreciation of their gift of insight into the times Carey had to see through others' eyes.

The reader gets the impression Carey sat down and wrote *Illywhacker*, the chapters flowing swiftly and easily like one of his Australian rivers in flood.

Every writer knows this would not be so, and to make it sound so, is no mean achievement.

That Eye The Sky

Fremantle Arts Review, vol. 1 no. 4, April 1986

Everyone who lives in Western Australia or visits there knows the sky is different. It seems closer to the earth, sometimes the clouds above that brooding, changing landscape seem close enough to touch.

Tim Winton, the youthful West Australian who has the midas touch when it comes to literary awards (the Miles Franklin, the West Australian Council Week Literary Award, the Australia/Vogel Award), has given the sky an all-seeing eye in his latest book, *That Eye The Sky*.

But perhaps it is simply Winton who has projected his own bright sharp eye to a watching post to observe a family of ordinary people caught up in the wilderness of the 80s, witnessing the clash of cultures and the gaps in the generations wider than those in the walls of their mean little house on the outskirts of a mean little place called Bankside.

Morton Flack, the narrator of the story, is a boy of eleven depending largely on the cracks and the keyholes and the doors that don't fully close to learn about life.

The cracks and the keyholes play a major role in the story. Through them with an ear as sharp as the eye young Ort gathers a bountiful supply of life's facts, enough to destroy his innocence.

By this means he hears the life story of Henry Warburton, a strange, one-eyed mix-up of a man, currently a wandering evangelist who wandered into the Flack home. His life up to now was a series of tragedies, his teaching career unfairly curtailed, his family wiped out in an accident, his father a high churchman who rebuffed him.

This is the book's weakness. Few life stories would

come out so evenly and coherently through a crack in a door, even allowing for the super intelligence of young Ort, camouflaged much of the time by the wistful, childish candour, a quality that is guaranteed to make every female reader of the adult age want him for their own.

Henry Warburton does not evoke the same sympathy despite his hard life, and had I been reading *That Eye The Sky* strictly for pleasure (and Winton is certainly pleasurable reading) I would have skipped his religious ravings, often taking up large hunks of space.

On the other hand Ort's older sister Tegwyn, a rebellious teenager as mixed up in her own way as Warburton in his, comes sympathetically to life. She hardly utters a pleasant word, but you care deeply about her, and know there is a warmth inside her shapely young body stifled by her anger at life's rough deal. Her mother explains her behaviour to Ort. "Kids hate everything when they're sixteen. Even themselves."

Through Tegwyn Winton shows us that while times change people don't. Alice Flack (the mother) rebelled too at her age and wandered from the beaten track of the Establishment, met Sam (the father) who asked no more from life than some trees to live amongst.

Sam is the victim of a car accident in the opening pages of *That Eye The Sky* which turns the Flack world upside down until Warburton appears to give it some sort of shaky order. Winton keeps the reader titillated wondering if it will be Tegwyn or Alice, lonely and sexually deprived since Sam's accident, who will ultimately give bed room to Warburton. Again the keyhole provides the answer.

Winton himself, in his mid-twenties, is distanced between the father and son, painting them both with an artist's skill of stepping back to focus them clearly. You suffer for Sam, seeing him before the accident that crippled him, vibrant with life, his hair in a long plait down his back as Winton sometimes wears his own. The young Ort, so totally committed to love, must be a part of the young Winton, himself (we are told) part of a loving, caring family.

A senile grandmother completes the Flack household. She spent much of her early life with a transient husband, enlivening a dreary existence by playing the piano. Once she flung out a fist and broke up a fight keeping the keys going with the other hand.

Winton's writing is rather like that. The lyrics are combined with the harsh realities.

"Sometimes Fat and me lie under there (a wooden bridge) in the cool with all the insects singing and listen to the cars going across, seeing all the boards going like a xylophone. There's a high note at one end and a low one at the other. Cars come up the scales or down them."

The young Ort milks the family cow.

"Sunday morning. It's cool. Summer is about over. Margaret makes ork, pork, goilk noises in her guts. Her milk comes out hard and thin and makes the bucket growl."

That Eye The Sky is Winton's third major work since *An Open Summer* in 1980. One wonders what is yet to come from his pen. He might well continue writing for another forty years. What will he think of *That Eye The Sky* then? Perhaps like a great many other writers viewing their early work, he will cast it off with embarrassment. Maybe not. Like the young Ort he might maintain his love for all creations.

I hope he never sees Henry Warburton again.

NOTES ON SOURCES

Primary sources used include: Jennifer Ellison, ed., *Rooms of Their Own*, Ringwood: Penguin, 1986, 214-29; Daniel Connell, *The War at Home*, ABC Enterprises, 1988; Mary Wright interview, *Fremantle Arts Review*, June 1987; Deborah Tarrant interview, *Weekend Australian Magazine*, 15-16 October 1983; Michael Cordell, *Sydney Morning Herald* Weekend Magazine, 15 September 1984; Ruth Dewsbury, *Sydney Morning Herald Good Weekend*, 18 May 1987; *Wollongong Advertiser*, 28 May 1986; Stuart Sayers, "Writers and Readers", The *Age*, October 1984; the *Newcastle Herald*, 1 June 1985; "The Coming Out Show: The Legacies Of Olga Masters", Australian Women's Broadcasting Cooperative, ABC National Radio, September 1988, producers Kate Veitch and Janet Parker; Fr. A. Havas, *History of the Cobargo Parish 1829-1984*; Chris Wallace-Crabbe, "Lost in Wonderland", *Scripsi*, vol. 4, no. 1, July 1986, 163-171; *Soviet Literature*, May 1985 and April 1986 issues; Olga Masters' official report on the Russian tour, 29 November 1985, in papers held by the Literature Board of the Australia Council; Blanche d'Alpuget, "Why Mother Russia Still Weeps", *Good Weekend*, 24 September 1988; "Country Press" by Rosemary Dobson in *Selected Poems*, North Ryde: Angus and Robertson, 1973; *Con-*

temporary Authors, Detroit: Gale Research, 1962-, vol. 121, 1987, 286-87; Tom Thompson in *The View from Tinsel Town*, Southerly: Penguin, 1985, 42-46; Constance Larmour, "Women's Wages and the WEB [Women's Employment Board]", *Labour History* no. 29, 1975, 47-48; four ABC Radio interviews with Alison Cotes, Pru Goward, Halina Scezcyk and Jill Kitson.

Secondary sources include: Dorothy Jones, "Drama's Vitallest Expression: The Fiction of Olga Masters", *Australian Literary Studies*, vol. 13, May 1987, 3-14, and "Digging Deep: Olga Masters, Storyteller", *Kunapipi*, vol. 8, no. 3, 1986, 28-35; Jill Matthews, *Good and Mad Women: The Historical Construction of Femininity in Twentieth Century Australia*, Sydney: Allen and Unwin, 1984; K.M. Reiger, *The Disenchantment of the Home: Modernizing the Australian Family, 1880-1940*, Melbourne: Oxford University Press, 1985; Ann Game and Rosemary Pringle, "The Making of the Australian Family", *Intervention*, vol. 12, 1979, 63-83; R.B. Walker, *Yesterday's News: A History of the Newspaper Press in NSW from 1920 to 1945*, Sydney: Sydney University Press, 1980.